Praise for  bo

"Thanks to Wolff and friends, the cyberswamp may just have become a little less murky."
—*Entertainment Weekly*

"*NetGuide* is the computer world's online *TV Guide*®."
—*Good Morning America*

"*NetGuide* will keep you from wandering around aimlessly on the Internet, and is full of good ideas for where to pull over."
—*Forbes FYI*

"*NetGuide* is the liveliest, most readable online guide yet."
—*USA Today*

"What you need to connect."—*Worth Magazine*

"*NetGuide* is the *TV Guide*® to Cyberspace!"
—Louis Rossetto, publisher/editor, *Wired*

"One of the more complete, well-organized guides to online topics. From photography to the Church of Elvis, you'll find it here."
—*PC Magazine*

"The best attempt yet at categorizing and organizing all the great stuff you can find out there. It's the book people keep stealing off my desk."—Joshua Quittner, *New York Newsday*

"It's changed my online life. Get this book!"
—Mike Madson, "Computer Bits," Business Radio Network

"My favorite for finding the cool stuff."
—*The Louisville Courier-Journal*

"*NetGuide* focuses on the most important aspect of online information—its content. You name it, it's there—from erotica to religion to politics."—Lawrence J. Magid, *San Jose Mercury News*

"Not only did all the existing Net books ignore Cyberspace's entertaining aspects, but they were process-oriented, not content-oriented. Why hadn't someone made a *TV Guide*® for the Net? Wolff recognized an opportunity for a new book, and his group wrote *NetGuide*."—Mark Frauenfelder, *Wired*

"Couch potatoes have *TV Guide*®. Now Net surfers have *NetGuide*."—*Orange County Register*

"*NetGuide* is one of the best efforts to provide a hot-spot guide to going online."—*Knoxville News-Sentinel*

"Assolutamente indispensabile!"—*L'Espresso*, Italy

"A valuable guide for anyone interested in the recreational uses of personal computers and modems."
—Peter H. Lewis, *The New York Times*

"*NetGames* is a good map of the playing fields of Netdom."
—*Newsweek*

"This guide to games people play in the ever-expanding Cyberspace shows you exactly where to go."
—*Entertainment Weekly*

"The second book in a very good series from Wolff and Random House."—Bob Schwabach, syndicated columnist

"Hot addresses!"—*USA Weekend*

"Move over Parker Brothers and Nintendo—games are now available online. There's something in *NetGames* for everyone from crossword-puzzle addicts to Dungeons & Dragons fans."
—*Reference Books Bulletin*

"Whether you're a hardened game player or a mere newbie, *NetGames* is the definitive directory for gaming on the Internet."
—*.net*

"A wide and devoted following."—*The Wall Street Journal*

"*NetMoney* is a superb guide to online business and finance!"
—*Hoover's Handbook of American Business*

"[*NetChat*] is...the best surfer's guide out there."
—*Entertainment Weekly*

"A product line of guidebooks for explorers of the Internet."
—*Inside Media*

Neither *NetGuide* nor Wolff New Media LLC is affiliated with, sponsored, nor endorsed by *TV Guide*® or its publishers.

INSTANT

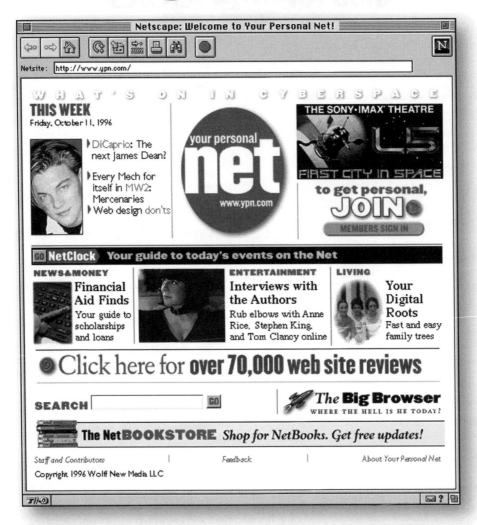

Visit Your Personal Net at

UPDATES

WOLFF NEW MEDIA

The NetBooks Series is published by Wolff New Media LLC, 520 Madison Avenue, 11th Floor, New York, NY 10022, and distributed by National Book Network, 4720 Boston Way, Lanham, MD 20706, as agent for Wolff New Media LLC.

NetKids has been wholly created and produced by Wolff New Media LLC. *NetKids, NetShopping, NetSci-Fi, NetSpy, NetCollege, NetStudy, NetDoctor, NetMarketing, NetVote, NetJobs, NetGames2, NetTravel, NetTaxes, NetMusic, NetGames, NetChat, NetMoney, NetTech, NetSports,* Your Personal Net, the Your Personal Net Logo, NetBooks, NetHead, NetSpeak, NetBest, and CyberPower are trademarks of Wolff New Media LLC. The Net Logo, What's On In Cyberspace, and YPN are registered trademarks of Wolff New Media LLC. All design and production has been done by means of desktop-publishing technology. The text is set in the typefaces Champion, Century 725, Dolores, Eldorado, Funhouse, and Improv.

Published simultaneously in the U.S. and Canada by Wolff New Media LLC

0 9 8 7 6 5 4 3 2 1

ISBN 1-889670-08-1

The authors and publisher have used their best efforts in preparing this book. However, the authors and publisher make no warranties of any kind, express or implied, with regard to the documentation contained in this book, and specifically disclaim, without limitation, any implied warranties of merchantability and fitness for a particular purpose with respect to listings in the book, or the techniques described in the book. In no event shall the authors or publisher be responsible or liable for any loss of profit or any other commercial damages, including but not limited to special, incidental, consequential, or any other damages in connection with or arising out of furnishing, performance, or use of this book.

All of the photographs and illustrations in this book have been obtained from online sources, and have been included to demonstrate the variety of work that is available on the Net. The caption with each photograph or illustration identifies its online source. Text and images available over the Internet and other online services may be subject to copyright and other rights owned by third parties. Online availability of text and images does not imply that they may be reused without the permission of rights holders, although the Copyright Act does permit certain unauthorized reuse as fair use under 17 U.S.C. §107. Care should be taken to ensure that all necessary rights are cleared prior to reusing material distributed over the Internet and other online services. Information about reuse is available from the institutions that make their materials available online.

Trademarks

A number of entered words in which we have reason to believe trademark, service mark, or other proprietary rights may exist have been designated as such by use of initial capitalization. However, no attempt has been made to designate as trademarks or service marks all personal-computer words or terms in which proprietary rights might exist. The inclusion, exclusion, or definition of a word or term is not intended to affect, or to express any judgment on, the validity or legal status of any proprietary right which may be claimed in that word or term.

Manufactured in the United States of America.

New York

WOLFF NEW MEDIA

Michael Wolff
Publisher and Editor in Chief

Kelly Maloni
Executive Editor

Stevan Keane
Editor

Stephen Gullo
Creative Director

Research Editor: Kristin Miller
Senior Editor: Dina Gan
Managing Editor: Donna Spivey

Design Director of NetKids: Sandra Schmitt

Associate Art Director: Eric Hoffsten
Associate Design Director: Marya Triandafellos
Assistant Art Director: Jay Jaffe
Contributing Illustrator: Nancy Wolff

Editor of NetKids: Bennett Voyles

Associate Editors: Deborah Cohn, Lev Grossman,
Hylton Jolliffe
Staff Writers: Henry Lam, Wendy Nelson,
Stephanie Overby
Copy Editors: Sonya Donaldson, Candice Luce
Editorial Assistants: Jennifer Levy, Vicky Tsolomytis
Research Assistants: Max Greenhut, Rachel Kleinman
Production Assistants: Alex Fogarty, Jackie Fugere,
Gary Gottshall, Rob Hardin, Jennie Nichols, Peter Rinzler

Special thanks:
NetResponse—Tom Feegel, Richard Mintz, Adam Behrens, Luis Babicek, Bob Bachle, Max Cacas, Cheryl Gnehm, Paul Hinkle, Larry Kirk, Chris Quillian, Jonathan Rouse, Brent Sleeper, and Pete Stein
And, as always, Aggy Aed
The editors of *NetKids* can be reached at Wolff New Media LLC, 520 Madison Avenue, 11th Floor, New York, NY 10022, or by voice call at 212-308-8100, fax at 212-308-8837, or email at editors@ypn.com.

KIDS RULE THE NET

The only guide to the Internet written by kids

A MICHAEL WOLFF BOOK

WOLFF NEW MEDIA

New York

NetKids

Table of Contents

NetKids FAQ

1 What can a kid do on the Internet?

You can make friends with kids in other states and other countries. You can play games. You can find information for school reports, or look at great pictures of animals just for fun. You can read about your favorite singer, movie star, or pro athlete, or listen to sounds from your favorite cartoons. You can look at pictures of stars, planets, and space ships, and find out what qualifications you need to become an astronaut. Whatever you're interested in, you can find out more about it on the Internet—and if you follow our instructions carefully, you should be able to do most of it yourself.

2 Why should I trust this guide?

The reviews in this guide were written by kids like you. They might not always share your interests, and you may not always agree with them, but you know they're telling you the truth. They're not teachers trying to talk you into liking a subject or parents who want you to eat your cyberspinach. You're getting the straight story.

3 What is the Internet, anyway?

The Internet is a network of computers all over the world. When you log onto the Internet, your computer becomes part of that network. It turns your computer into a kind of phone, but much better than a phone, because you can get written information, computer programs, and pictures as well as sound.

4. Is the Internet the same thing as the World Wide Web?

The World Wide Web is the newest part of the Internet, but it's the part that's most popular right now. What makes the Web different from the older parts of the Internet is that it's more colorful and has an easier way of getting from site to site called hypertext. With hypertext, you just click on a highlighted word and wham! you're there. If you're looking at a Disney site and see *The Lion King* highlighted, you just click, and you're at a Lion King site.

5. How about America Online? Is that the Internet, too?

America Online is a commercial online service that has its own separate network, but people who subscribe can also send email and look at the Web.

6. Everything takes a long time to load. What causes that?

The Web is still very new, and not all the bugs are worked out yet. Unfortunately, it's also very slow. The problem is not the Web so much as the size of the wire to your phone. The data stream is moving very quickly out on the fat main lines, but when it gets on the skinny wire to your home phone, it has to slow down to a trickle.

7 How can I speed things up?

In a few years, everything will be hundreds of times faster. For now, the best we can suggest is that you get a 28.8 Kbps modem and have something handy to do while you wait. If your computer is big enough, you may even want to play a game and then switch back to your first browser window when it's loaded (or write a note to your granchildren about the pace of life on the electronic frontier, circa 1996!). One more tip: Sometimes, the fault may not be with your telephone line but with an especially slow site. When that happens, try opening a second browser (on Netscape, select New Browser) and surf elsewhere while www.molasses.org oozes down to your machine.

8 What's a Web site?

A Web site is kind of like a magazine, except that instead of just being able to turn pages, you can also download short movies, play games, listen to music, or even talk to people who are visiting the same site. Not all sites have all those things, of course, but the webmasters (the people who design Web pages) can choose to use one or more of those elements.

9 What's a home page?

It's your own personal Web site. It's where you put art, stories, or just favorite links you'd like to share. It can be anything at all really.

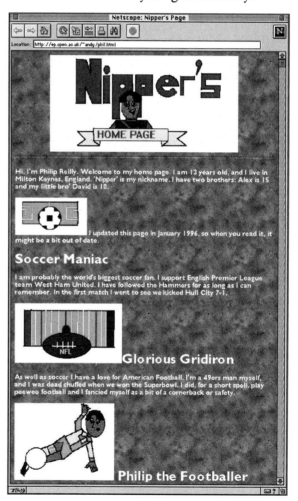

10 Will I need a browser?

Definitely. A browser is a program that lets you look at the World Wide Web. The most popular one right now is Netscape Navigator, with Microsoft Explorer a distant second. Both work in the same way. There's a space in the top where you can insert the address you want (if you're working from a book), or in which an address will appear if you click on highlighted text or a button (if you're getting somewhere using hypertext). There is also a series of buttons that help you control what you see as well, the most important of which is BACK, which sends you back to the last page you've seen. Your Internet provider will probably give you a browser when you sign up.

11 What's a bookmark?

It's an address you've saved on your browser. If you like a site a lot, you can let your browser save the address so you won't have to retype it or look for it the next time you're on the Web. You'll just pull down the menu, click, and go.

Stevan Keane,10:08 PM 10/12/96,NetKids

Subject: NetKids

X-Sender: skeane@merlin.netresponse.com
Mime-Version: 1.0
Date: Sat, 12 Oct 1996 22:08:11 -0500
To: hoffsten@ypn.com
From: skeane@ypn.com (Stevan Keane)
Subject: NetKids

Eric
I can't believe we're still in the office at 10pm on a Saturday night working on this book! Anyway, I've put the files you requested in the relevant folders and we'll be finding a Kids' homepage picture for the backcover really soon.

Stevan

Stevan Keane
Editor
Wolff New Media
New York, NY, 10022,
skeane@ypn.com, tel 212-833 0828, fax 212-833 8837

"I'm one tough gazookas, Which hates all palookas, Who ain't on the ups and square, I biffs em
and boffs em, And Always outroughs em, And none of em gets nowhere."
Albert Camus

---

12 Should I be careful?

Yes, but if you're smart you don't have to worry. Don't give out very personal information, and never give your home address or phone number without your parents' permission. If something seems strange to you, or if someone is bothering you, you can always leave. It's like the phone—if somebody's cursing at you or making you feel uncomfortable, all you have to do is hang up. In the end, your brain is your best defense.

13 What is email?

Email is an electronic message system that lets you send and receive electronic messages with anyone in the world who has an email address. It's easier than writing letters because you don't have to worry about stamps and mailboxes. It's also very fast. You can either use a separate mail program or use the mail program included as part of your browser. If you have an Internet account, you definitely have an email address.

14 How do I find a site on a subject that's not listed in this book?

Easy! Go to a search engine. You can choose either a specific search engine for kids (Yahooligans! is one), or the more general search engines. Remember in the old *Star Trek* when Captain Kirk asks the computer for information about something, and the computer gets it? A search engine is a bit like that. You just type in words that have to do with the subject you're interested in, hit enter, and the search engine looks all over for sites that match those words. A new screen pops up with a list of Web addresses that either have those words or are on the subject you want to find out more about.

15 Which search engine should I use?

There are a number of search engines around, and David Lindsay, 11, of Calgary, Canada, has reviewed a bunch of them for you in the box that begins on the next page. He's also included some great searching tips.

Alta Vista

http://www.altavista.com

Alta Vista, strangely, is not exactly a well-known search engine, compared to our other contenders, like Webcrawler, Infoseek, and Yahoo! even though it is one of the better ones. However, Alta Vista is expected to soon become one of the bigger search engines. It has just as many features as any other search engine, including tips on searching (which everyone should take a look at before navigating the Web) contests, and of course, a store where you can purchase items online. Searching with Alta Vista is very fast and accurate.

Hot Tip:

When searching, try to use the search engine's own site address rather than using the Net Search button at the Netscape info bar—Net Search is filled with more images for all the different search engines, so it takes longer for it to load. You may have to wait longer for your search results.

Excite

http://www.excite.com

Excite is one of the neatest search engines anywhere. It is very easy to understand. It usually runs at a pretty moderate speed, but sometimes it will run faster, and sometimes very slow. There is a weekly cartoon drawn by Bill Mitchell. The cartoon's usually a political joke, so bear in mind, if it makes no sense, maybe you should read the newspaper. Excite is relatively accurate. Much like Lycos, Yahoo!, and Infoseek, you can search different categories (The Web, Reviews, etc).

Infoseek

http://www.infoseek.com

Infoseek is a very well-known search engine, and for a good reason: They index pages under every word inside of it, rather than some words, so it's much more accurate. Infoseek is by far the most accurate search engine. It also has a page filled with helpful search tips. If you're searching for info on pythons but not *Monty Python,* you would type "Python -Monty" and anything with Monty in it wouldn't be found. You can even search for sites that are only "select sites" that have been nominated by Infoseek.

Lycos
http://www.lycos.com

Lycos boasts of being the largest search engine on the Internet. It has nearly 51.2 million Internet addresses. Searching is decently acurrate on Lycos. It takes a little longer to get your results from Lycos than the other Search Engines, but you get a high-percentage acurracy rate, and it even highlights all the keywords in the results.

WebCrawler
http://www.webcrawler.com

WebCrawler is one of the more unique search engines: It has every feature from taking you to random Web sites, to making a button for your page that's for finding other related links. WebCrawler, which is also known as "The Fastest Search on the Web," and also lives up to that name. WebCrawler may not be the most accurate

search engine, but it is definitely the least time-consuming. If time is not a concern, you can tell WebCrawler to give you a summary of each site listed—about 30 words long per site.

Hot Tip:

If speed is a big concern, tell WebCrawler to list the titles, and it will search even faster!

Yahoo!
http://www.yahoo.com

Yahoo! may not be the most accurate Search Engine in the world—"Redwall," a normally huge topic (over 100 sites) showed nothing on Yahoo! Speed is fairly good on Yahoo! but not as good as it could be. There are too many images, and too many ads that take up a lot of space, that slows it down a little.

David Lindsay, 11, Calgary, Canada

16 When I go to a search engine, I just get these long lists and I don't find anything. Is there an easier way?

Using search engines takes practice and a little patience. Instead, you may want to try using one of the sites that offers reviews of Web sites, not just the search engines that spit out names and addresses. Two of the best are the Point, at www.pointcom.com, and Your Personal Net, at www.ypn.com. YPN is produced by Wolff New Media, the publisher of *NetKids*. Both these sites have short reviews written by professional writers who let you know what you'll find at a given site and whether it's worth a visit. YPN, for example, has more than 70,000 reviews, covering many different topics.

17 How do I get sound and movies on my computer?

More and more, sound and video applications are being built right into computer operating systems and browsers, and chances are you already have at least some of the software you need already. Unfortunately, because the Web is so new, you will still sometimes try to download a movie and be told you can't because you need a special plug-in. Don't worry. If you have a newer computer with speakers, you should be in good shape. Most of the time you won't even have to buy anything.

Plug-Ins

A plug-in is just a piece of software that can be added to your browser. It allows your computer to "read" a new kind of file (a movie file, for example). Right now, most plug-ins are free because the software developers are competing with one another to have their plug-in become the movie player or sound player that everybody uses. Some developers may start charging for their plug-ins later on, but it seems likely that more of them hope to make money from charging site makers rather than site users.

everything from a baseball game in San Francisco to the Top 40 in Hong Kong—often live. There are now nearly 1,000 sites that have RealAudio, and more than 100 radio stations that broadcast live. It can be downloaded as www.realaudio.com.

ShockWave

The main reason you'll want this plug-in is it allows you to play interactive games on some of the slicker Web sites, especially movie sites. This can be downloaded at www.macromedia.com/shockwave.

QuickTime

This is probably the most common movie player. It's the first one you'll want to get, anyway. It's Apple-invented software, but there are versions available for both Mac and Windows, both of which can be downloaded at www.quicktime.apple.com.

Downloading a plug-in is easy, but you have to follow the instructions exactly once it's on your desktop. It's a good project to do with someone you know who's good with computers, at least the first time. There are many plug-ins out there, but the ones we like most are:

RealAudio

This lets you listen to special RealAudio files, as well as to radio stations all over the world. The great thing about RealAudio is that it allows you to listen to special sound files without downloading them. You can tune in to

Chapter 1

World's a Zoo

i think ANY kid, no matter what their interests or age, would enjoy the Internet! There are games to download, pictures to download, stories to read, people to chat with, info on your favorite movies & TV shows, and the list goes on and on. ANYTHING you want, you'll find it on the Net. There's stuff for little kids right up to old folk. I've even seen dogs and cats home pages!
Who'd a thunk it?

Nykki-Lynn
Smelser 10
LONDON, ONTARIO, CANADA

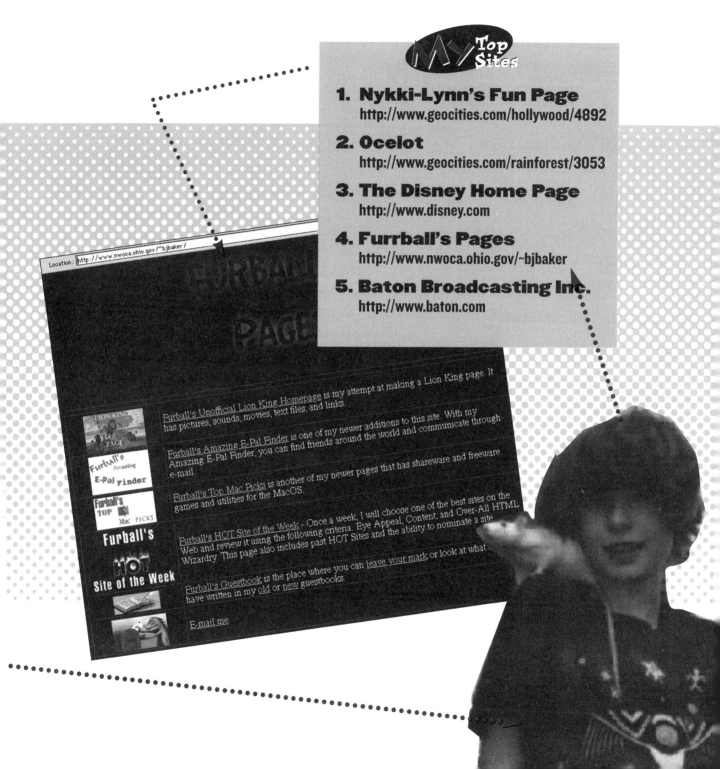

My Top Sites

1. **Nykki-Lynn's Fun Page**
   http://www.geocities.com/hollywood/4892

2. **Ocelot**
   http://www.geocities.com/rainforest/3053

3. **The Disney Home Page**
   http://www.disney.com

4. **Furrball's Pages**
   http://www.nwoca.ohio.gov/~bjbaker

5. **Baton Broadcasting Inc.**
   http://www.baton.com

Location: http://www.nwoca.ohio.gov/~bjbaker/

Furball's Unofficial Lion King Homepage is my attempt at making a Lion King page. It has pictures, sounds, movies, text files, and links.

Furball's Amazing E-Pal Finder is one of my newer additions to this site. With my Amazing E-Pal Finder, you can find friends around the world and communicate through e-mail.

Furball's Top Mac Picks is another of my newer pages that has shareware and freeware games and utilities for the MacOS.

Furball's HOT Site of the Week - Once a week, I will choose one of the best sites on the Web and review it using the following criteria: Eye Appeal, Content, and Over-All HTML Wizardry. This page also includes past HOT Sites and the ability to nominate a site.

Furball's Guestbook is the place where you can leave your mark or look at what have written in my old or new guestbooks

E-mail me

Monkeys & Apes

Do you like bananas? Want to meet your closest relatives? Come and join these tree-swinging, fruit-munching, hairy online apes and monkeys

Smelly Showdown

During a "stink fight," lemurs raise their tails over their heads and jab the end towards their opponents until one backs down. These fights are called "stink fights" because the lemurs have scent glands that spread throughout the tail during grooming. The scent glands are also used to mark branches in the lemur troop's territory.

The Ring-Tailed Lemur
http://rdserv1.rd.msu.edu /zoo/end/lemur/default.htm

African Primates at Home Home Page

If you're keen on primates, you'll go ape over this Web site. It has facts and figures on all species of primates from chimpanzees to gorillas, so whether you need the info for your homework assignment or are just interested, this page should sate you. If you delve deeper into the site you may stumble upon on-going research into human right and left handedness, which you can participate in.
http://www.indiana.edu/~primate/primates.html
Philip Reilly, 12

Zoo Primates

Zoo Primates is an excellent site for kids interested in exploring the many animals in nature. If you click on the name of an animal, it shows its picture and some facts. You learn many new things! One of the best parts is the "African Rain Forest" section. The only thing this site is missing is the beautiful colors of a real zoo. I guess they want you to imagine them.
http://caboose.com/altopics/portland_zoo/maingate/primates
Kelly Roman, 11

Primate Gallery

This site has some interesting facts, including where monkeys live and can be found. There are lots of funny-looking monkeys with goofy tails. Some have very strange faces. It is also fun to hear the sounds monkeys and apes make.
http://www.selu.com/~bio/PrimateGallery
Susanna Wolff, 8

About Those Gorillas...

Gorillas are probably man's closest animal relative. At the Gorilla Foundation, people are trying to teach them to communicate with us through sign language. Learn all about these amazing creatures at this Web site. It has pictures of the three gorillas that are being taught sign language, and a chart that tells about their favorite toys, books, movies, and many other things. This site is very informative, as well as nicely organized.
http://www.gorilla.org/Gorillas/#personal
Katie Tandler, 13

Location: http://www.gorilla.org/PhotoVideo/Koko_w_Penny_Smoky.jpg

Q: How's the Weather Up There?

A: Orangutans are the largest tree-dwelling animals in the world. They can spend their days swinging from branch to branch, 20 feet in the air, but that does not mean they have the ability to land on their feet, like cats. In fact, falling could be fatal for an orangutan, so their bodies evolved in a way to prevent it. They have developed incredible upper body strength and long, narrow hands and feet, to make it easy to grab and hold on to branches.

Orangutan Facts
http://www.ns.net /orangutan/facts.html

Big Cats

With the grace of house cats and the power of bears, big cats are the nobility of the animal kingdom—if the nobility chased down its prey and ripped it apart with its claws, that is

K nown as the "king" of beasts, the lion possesses great strength in his forebody. The only other cat with comparable strength is the tiger. And his roar is so powerful, the force can actually raise a cloud of dust.

Lion Facts
http://www.servtech.com
/public/lionlamb/lionfact.html

Jungle Cats

If you're doing a school report on lions, tigers, or leopards, this is the first Web site to visit. Compare the growls of a lion with those of a tiger. Download a picture, or learn fun facts. (Did you know that a tiger is about 20 percent larger than a lion?) There are also links to several other sites on the big cats. Jungle Cats is part of a larger site called "Jungle Animals."
http://greeceny.com/proj/cats.html
David Lindsay, 11

Five Tigers

This great conservation site has lots of links and addresses to other tiger sites or those specializing in a certain breed. The simple graphics are nice and well-presented. The kids' section is very interesting. There are lots of simplified facts, kids' tiger art and photos, video clips, and sound. Learn about all types of tigers with this nice, informative site.
http://www.5tigers.org
Hayley Morgan, 12

Tiger

Tiger Facts

Animal lovers will adore this site. Information includes a description of tigers, threats upon them, and most importantly, what you can do to help. For one thing, you might join the WWF (World Wildlife Fund) to help protect endangered species of tigers and other animals. If more information is required then there are plenty of links to environmental matters. Tigers are not the only creatures featured in this site. Fact sheets on other animals are included—great school project data.

http://www.wwfcanada.org/facts/tiger.html
Rachel Prior, 11

Faster Than a Speeding Sports Car

The cheetah can probably accelerate to 55 mph faster than your family's car, unless someone in your family is driving a Ferrari. A cheetah goes from 0 to 55 mph in 3 seconds! These cats have the reputation of being the most effective hunters in Africa.

Cheetahs
http://www.bhm.tis.net/zoo/animals/cheetah.html

The Safari

Going on an African or Asian safari isn't all fun and games—some of it is aardvark! And elephants, and rhinos, and hippos, and zebras...

An Aardvark in Shining Armor

If you were to pass a pangolin in Africa or the Near and Far East, you would probably think you were strolling by a pine cone. Unless you noticed its legs. In which case, you would probably assume you were passing a pine cone with legs. This is because of the pangolin's scaly epidermal armor. In a two-word definition, they are scaly anteaters. Lacking teeth, these animals have long and scaly tongues. The muscular roots of a pangolin's tongue is attached to its pelvis!

The Pangolin
http://www.infoweb.co.za /enviro/stories/pangolin.htm

Hippos

What lives in the sub-Saharan Africa area and weighs 1,300 to 3,250 kilograms? You guessed it! The hippopotamus. Find out about its habitats, how much grass it can eat in one bite, and about its really long life. This site has a neat picture of a hippo at the top of the page.
http://ape.apenet.it/EDV/ZOO/AN_TERRA/e_ippopotamo.html
Joe Conrad, 13

More About Rhinos

This site doesn't have any pictures, but it is still interesting. It contains tons of information pertaining to the rhinos, everything from behavior and survival methods to protection from poachers. For example, did you know that black and white rhinos have no biting teeth?
http://www.hull.ac.uk/Hull /pub_web/scrap.html
Melissa Edwards, 14

Meet Our Elephants

Did you know an elephant can eat 495 lbs (225 kg) of food and drink 50 gals (190 litres) of water per day? How would you like to get your last tooth when you were 40 years old? Well, here you can meet Zimba, now living in Byteme Zoo after retirement from 40 years with the circus. Hear her roar and see pictures of her. There is also lots of interesting information on these enormous creatures.

http://www.seas.gwu.edu/student/hurstd/elephant.html
Nykki-Lynn Smelser, 10

Zebra

Zebras, killed by man for their coats, are just one of the endangered species featured here. Read about other animals from around the world in danger of extinction. For example, Australia's koala bears, South America's parrots, and Africa's cheetahs. Other animals talked about include giraffes, bald eagles, jaguars, killer and humpback whales, and the list goes on. While here, test your environmental knowledge or join E.Patrol for the preservation of endangered animals.

http://www.sprint.com/epatrol/afzebra.html
Nykki-Lynn Smelser, 10

Q: Do elephants ever forget?

A: An elephant's memory is similar to other intelligent mammals. This means that elephants do have a good memory, but not any better or worse than dogs, cats, or humans. Sometimes, like dogs, trained elephants will forget the meaning of "come here," if they are busy, or "go away," if you're holding a banana.

Frequently Asked Questions About Elephants
http://www.wineasy.se /elephant/consult/faq.htm

Bugs, Bugs, Bugs, Bugs

These bugs are exactly where you would expect to find them. They're all caught in a World Wide Web! There are sites on just about every insect you could name, and some you couldn't

Trivia

The world's largest roach is six inches long—with a one-foot wingspan!

Cockroach World
http://www.nj.com/yucky /roaches/index.html

Ants communicate by touch and smell. When they find food, they lay down a chemical trail so other ants will be able to find their way back to the source.

Ask Orkin: Ants
http://www.orkin.com/orkin /page6.html

Dr. Don's Termite Pages

If you like termites, you should definitely visit this page. It has a whole bunch of information on termites. It has some pictures of termite mounds and such information as who runs the colony, how to avoid termite problems, and how to choose a pest controller. It also has some links to other termite pages.

http://www.wark.csiro.au/ewart/tp_g.htm

Emily Malloch, 11

Africanized Honey Bees Home Page

Find out about dangerous bees here. You will learn about killer-bee history here and how only a scientist can tell them from good honey bees. By clicking around on this nice site I learned how beekeepers are worried about them coming here.

http://128.194.30.1/agcom/news/hc/ahb/ahbhome.htm

Amy Schroeder, 10

Cockroach World

This is one of the coolest sites on the Net, with lots of interesting and educational facts about cockroaches, presented in an entertaining format. What's a day in the life of a cockroach like? You can find out here! This site is filled with images of cockroaches, .WAV sound files of real roaches, and even a game where you're given a description of a roach and a .WAV file of what it sounds like, and your task is to figure out where it's from. Even if you don't like roaches, this page can still help you out, as it also tells how to get rid of them!

http://www.nj.com/yucky/roaches/index.html

David Lindsay, 11

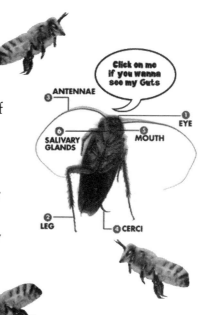

Click on me if you wanna see my Guts

③ ANTENNAE
① EYE
⑥ SALIVARY GLANDS
⑤ MOUTH
② LEG
④ CERCI

Those Thoughtful Termites

Termites will sometimes eat away at a wooden building's timbers, leaving the painted surface unchewed.

Ask Orkin: Termites
http://www.orkin.com /page1.html

Speedier Than the Shuttle

Fleas accelerate the equivalent of 50 times faster than a space shuttle does after liftoff—and can jump 150 times their length. That would be the same as a person jumping 1000 feet!

Ask Orkin: Fleas
http://www.orkin.com /page11.html

Starting a Butterfly Garden

By growing a butterfly's favorite plant, you can attract butterflies to your garden, in your backyard or on your windowsill.

Butterfly Garden
http://www.butterflies .com/garden.html

The Reptile House

Reptiles get a bad rap. Why are lizards used as ingredients in witches' spells? Why are most people scared of snakes? Find out if reptiles really deserve their reputations

Q: Is it true that some snakes "charm" their prey?

A: No, but sometimes their prey will become frozen with fear. This myth may have gotten started because sometimes animals will become frozen with fear when approached by a snake, and because snakes don't blink.

An Interactive Guide to Massachusetts Snakes
http://www.umass.edu/umext/snake

Everglades Alligator Farm

Read about a man by the name of Mr. John Hudson and his 'gator farm down in sunny Florida. Read about his struggle to keep the farm open. While you're there, visit the unique Gator Gift Store, where you can purchase alligator skin items and lots of other strange stuff. And then if you still are in need of 'gator facts, take the link to *Gator Times,* and read some more.
www.florida.com/gatorfarmer/index.html
Joe Conrad, 13

The Boa and Python Page

This page has links to nearly everything you want to know about boas. It has some cool pictures of boas. For just a boa page, it has quite a lot of information. It also includes lots of links, such as pictures of somebody's boas and some place where you can buy lizards and snakes.
http://laird.ccds.cincinnati.oh.us/%7Eschaefb
Danielle Jacovelli, 11

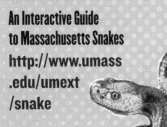

Snakes

If you enjoy snake venom, this is a field full of snakes for you! You can download a very large and disgusting picture of a snake. If you just happen to be visiting from Mars and you don't know what a snake is, it gives you the definition of a snake. Everything else is fangulous!

http://fovea.retina.net/~gecko/herps/snakes/index.shtml

Alex Landback, 10

Reptiles & Amphibians

Did you know that reptiles and amphibians are cold-blooded? Or what the biggest snake in the world is? Find the answers to your reptile/amphibian questions here! This site has a few paragraphs about these animals, and then tells all about the biggest snake in the world. At the bottom of the page, there are links off the same site about mammals, birds, and more.

http://sparky.cs.nyu.edu:19234/repti.html

Erin Fleege, 13

Who's More Scared?

If you're down South and happen to come across an alligator, be cautious. They have been known to attack, if they feel their babies are threatened. But although alligators can grow up to 15 feet long and weigh up to 1,300 pounds, they are wary of us. They see humans as bigger animals than themselves, and will usually leave them alone.

Alligator FAQ

http://plato.phy.ohiou.edu/~mash/herp/alligator.html

Cats & Dogs

Some may say a dog is man's best friend, but lots of cat lovers disagree. Either way, on the Internet it's always raining virtual cats and dogs

Oops!

In the late 1960s, cat breeders considered the first long-haired Abyssinian kittens to be "mistakes." In the United States, however, people taken with these long-haired "mistakes" began breeding them purposely and advancing until the breed became accepted for championship status.

Somali Breed FAQ
http://www
.fanciers
.com/breed
-faqs/somali
-faq.html

Myths and Facts About Cats

Myths and Facts About Cats is an interesting and fun page about cats! Did you know that cats don't always land on their feet? Or that cats actually CAN get rabies? These are some of the facts you're likely to find out here, along with many more myths and facts. If you're interested in cats, you should definitely check out this site.

http://www.cfainc.org/cfa/articles/myths-facts.html
Erin Fleege, 13

Feline Information Page

This is a very informative page about cats, lots to read about! You can look up feline history, nutrition, genetics, resources and more! Learn about Sir Lou, the cat, and admire a picture of the first Net-puss, Socks. These pages are simple, but packed with useful knowledge. There are only a few simple graphics, but this page is still pleasing to the eye. Purrrrrrrrfect!

http://www.best.com/~sirlou/cat.shtml
Hayley Morgan, 12

Location: http://sculptor.as.arizona.edu/foltz/bullys/polar.jpg

What Is a Frenchie?

This site has really cute pictures of bulldogs. Especially cute is a picture of a dog that looks like he has palm trees growing out of his head. There are lots of cute pictures.
http://www.bulldog.org/bullmarket
Susanna Wolff, 8

Cats, Cats, Cats!

If you are a cat person, this is the litter box for you. This person tells you about her pets. You can look at microscopic pictures of her pets or you can just download larger pictures of them.
http://www.rahul.net/hredlus/tales.html
Alex Landback, 10

The Truth About Cats & Dogs

Myth: Cats always land on their feet.

Fact: While cats instinctively fall feet first and may survive falls from high places, they also may receive broken bones in the process.

Myth: Animals heal themselves by licking their wounds.

Fact: Such licking actually can slow the healing process and further damage the wound.

Myth: A cat's sense of balance is in its whiskers.

Fact: Cats use their whiskers as "feelers" but actually use their tails to maintain their balance.

Myths and Facts About Cats
http://www.cfainc.org/cfa/articles/myths-facts.html

Dogs!

Happy Endings: Stories of Rescue Goldens

The most loved dogs now are invading cyberspace. Find out how you can own one, and possibly get it out of an abusive situation. This links to The Golden Retriever WWW Site, and some stories about people and the goldens they rescued.

http://www.rahul.net/ hredlus/tales.html

Joe Conrad, 13

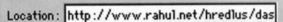

Location: http://www.rahul.net/hredlus/das

Location: http://www.rahul.net/hredlus

Location : http://www.rahul.net/hredlus/zwick3.gif

DOG

Location : http://www.rahul.n[   ]/C11.jpg

Dolphins & Whales

Dolphins and whales are intelligent and people-friendly mammals. Both species are be able to communicate across vast distances with their own kind and they don't even use email

Q: **Are whales mean?**

A: **Whales are wild animals, but the true whales are not predators . Some gray whales are actually so friendly that they have been known to come very close to whale watchers' boats—in some cases, close enough that they have let whale watchers pet them.**

Q: **Do you know what a baby whale is called when it is born?**

A: **A calf.**

Whale Times: Fishin' for Facts Library
http://www.whaletimes.org
/whafshn.ht

Location: http://www.ast.cam.ac.uk/~anj/dolphins/pair.gif

Dolphins and Man... Equals?

If you are really into dolphins, you should check out this site for some excellent research on how dolphins communicate. You might be surprised to find out just how intelligent dolphins are! There are some good pictures, links to more pictures, dolphin sounds, and a kid's dolphin chat line.
http://www.polaris.net/~rblacks/dolphins.htm
Andrea Bonilla, 13

Orcinus orca—Killer Whale

See the whales do very neat tricks in the water. One whale can do an even better backflip than my gymnastics teacher! My teacher can't do it without hands or flippers. On this site you can find out what killer whales eat—it's not people! Also, they don't eat their own kind.
http://www.slip.net/~oyafuso/orcinusorca.html
Susanna Wolff, 8

Whaletimes

This is one of the best whale pages on the Net. It has every-thing—facts, pictures, graphics, links, and environmental tips. It even has a kid version for the little surfers.
http://www.whaletimes.org/whagray.htm
Emily Malloch, 11

Whale Information Network

Wow! This page has everything. It has info on whales, facts on all different kinds of whales, and some links to other whale pages. It also has a link to Channel 9. The background on that page is definitely a downloader. To sum it all up, it's a whale of a page.
http://www.macmedia.com.au/whales
Emily Malloch, 11

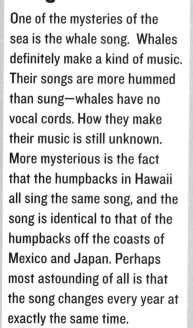

Ba ba ba, ba ba Beluga...

One of the mysteries of the sea is the whale song. Whales definitely make a kind of music. Their songs are more hummed than sung—whales have no vocal cords. How they make their music is still unknown. More mysterious is the fact that the humpbacks in Hawaii all sing the same song, and the song is identical to that of the humpbacks off the coasts of Mexico and Japan. Perhaps most astounding of all is that the song changes every year at exactly the same time.

The Song of the Whale
http://nko.mhpcc.edu/omi/omi_whalesong.html

Sharks

Sharks are predators, but they are not the monsters some movies would have us believe. Unless they are hungry, of course

The King of the Ocean

This page is all about white sharks. It has some nice pictures and lots of information on the sharks and how people have affected them. It's not very long and gets right to the point, a good page if you want the facts on white sharks.
http://www.mad-dog.net/sharks/sharksf.html
Emily Malloch, 11

Katie Hull's Shark & Sea

This is a pretty cool site. There is information about Katie, a 13-year-old who is very interested in sharks, and some cool stuff about sharks. Don't take the trivia test until you read the shark information or you may be unhappy with your score!
http://scubaworld.com/katie
Kelsey Mays, 11

Hammerhead Sharks

Do you like sharks? Not many people do. This site should be renamed as it expands past one type of shark. Do you know the difference between the Spiny Dog Fish Shark and the

Smooth Dog Fish Shark? Find out here. The pictures are realistic, clear, and sometimes sparkling. Links are simple and easy to follow. A recommended site to visit.
http://www.beach-net.com/Sharkhammer.html
Rachel Prior, 11

The Sharks! Site

All you ever wanted to know about sharks and much more. If you are one of the majority who thinks that sharks are bloodthirsty fish whose only aim in life is to eat anyone who gets in their way, YOU'RE WRONG. This page explains what sharks are, where they live, what they eat, why they attack people, and what you can do to protect them. If you really don't know much about sharks at all, there is a big intro which explains it all. A good page, and you don't have to be a sea-life lover to enjoy it.
http://www.io.org/~gwshark/sharks.html
Philip Reilly, 12

The Great White Shark Facts

This site gives a lot of neat info on the great white shark, such as why they haven't found fossils of great white sharks (because their bones are made of cartilage) and why a seal is more likely to be eaten by a great white shark than any other animal. The site has lots of neat pictures of the great white and its food. It even has a list of people attacked or killed by the great white shark.
http://www.netzone.com/~drewgrgich/picshark.html
Keith Miller, 8

Q: Are sharks fish?

A: Yes, but a special type of fish. They are classified in a group of creatures whose skeletons are made out of cartilage—a tough, rubbery material—rather than bone, like other fish. This category also includes rays, sawfish, and skates.

Fish FAQs.
http://www.wh.whoi.edu/faq/fishfaq8.html#q9

GET **T**H**i**S!

More people are killed each year by dogs than have been killed by white sharks in the last 100 years.

Animals
http://rgs.edu.sg/Animals/sharks.html

2 Time Machine

H ere are some reviews for my favorite sites.

1. Kidscom
http://www.kidscom.com
I like this site because it is ALL children-related. It has games, chat rooms, and craft ideas to keep us kids out of trouble.

2. MTV
http://www.mtv.com
It's a great site for one of the kids' favorite (and most watched) cable channel. It has links to read up on your favorite "video jockeys" and shows.

3. Yahooligans!
http://www.yahooligans.com
This is a page designed by Yahoo! It was especially made with kids in mind. It has links to kid-related sites, and even sites designed by kids!

Joe Conrad 13
oWOSSo, MiCHiGAN, USA

Thunder Lizards

Even though the word dinosaur means "thunder lizard" we still don't know what they really sounded like! Maybe they sounded like dogs. Rover lizards? Parrots? Polly lizards? Maybe so...

The Field Museum

This is a really neat site. It is great that you can find out about many different kinds of dinosaurs and extinct mammals. It has real pictures of fossils left from dinosaurs and extinct mammals and, if you have the right kind of computer, you can see and hear movies of dinosaurs and extinct mammals. There are good painted and drawn pictures on every page. This site has a lot of pictures but not enough writing.
http://rs6000.bvis.uic.edu:80/museum
Keith Miller, 8

Dinosaur Pictures

ROOOOAAARRR!!! Feeling brave? Then come to Dinosaur Pictures, a Web site like none other. At first, you see a list of dinosaurs. Double-click on one and watch a dinosaur appear on your screen! Although there's no color, the realistic backgrounds compensate. Oh yeah, and watch out for the Tyrannosaurus Rex!
http://aazk.ind.net/animal_gifs/Dinosaurs/Dinosaurs.html
Morgan Balavage, 12

Location: http://tyrrell.magtech.ab.ca/tour/trex2.jpg

Royal Tyrrell Museum

If you like dinosaurs here is the museum you've been waiting for! This page provides you with links to other dinosaur pages and has two large pictures of dinosaur skeletons. This page describes what the dinosaur looks like and who they were!
http://tyrrell.magtech.ab.ca/tour/dinohall.html
Alex Landback, 10

New Mexico Museum of Natural History and Science

Here is the virtual museum where you can find out a lot about dinosaurs and mammals of New Mexico. Read about the 150 million-year-old eggshell found here in October, 1995, or the first dinosaur skin found. And those are just a few of the things you can check out. Do you know what New Mexico's state fossil is (or that it even had one)? There's information on wild plants and fossils of all kinds as well as good teacher support pages.
http://www.aps.edu/HTMLPages/NMMNH.html
Nykki-Lynn Smelser, 10

Q: Is it true that not all the dinosaurs are extinct?

A: Don't look now, but one just flew by your window! After comparing bird and dinosaur skeletons, many biologists have concluded that birds are technically dinosaurs.

Berkeley Museum of Paleontology
http://ucmp.berkeley.edu

Q: What's a Cybersaurus?

A: Not a dinosaur with a modem for a tail! The Cybersaurus was actually a medium-sized dinosaur. It walked on two feet, weighed 180 pounds, and stood about six feet tall. It ate both plants and animals, and usually lived with other cyber-sauruses.

Berkeley Museum of Paleontology
http://ucmp.berkeley.edu
/trex/specialtrex2.html

The Pyramid People

They built the pyramids, they believed in an amazing afterlife, they lived thousands of years ago and, if you believe the pictures, they all walked sideways

Q: Were pharoahs always men?

A: Most, but not all. Two of the best-remembered, Nefertiti and Cleopatra, were women.

Q: What is the Egyptian Book of the Dead?

A: The Book of the Dead is a title used to describe a text used in funerals and placed in tombs. It was usually on papyrus and includes about two hundred spells.

Encyclopedia Smithsonian
http://www.si.edu/welcome/faq/pyramid.htm

Egypt Culturenet: Ancient

This site is a terrific idea for anyone who is interested in ancient Egyptian lifestyles. From the hieroglyphic alphabet to the lists of education and art resources this is great. On the down side, the page takes a long time to load... The page could definitely use more graphics that are eye-catching. The opening page only contains the text and title without any images. You may find it pretty dull. However, as you move on through the page, you will find a few more that pop out to grab your attention.

http://www.idsc.gov.eg/culture/anc.htm

Kellie Vaughn, 13

The Pharaoh's Challenge

Here's a challenging quiz on the Ancient Egyptians. Think you know it all? Try to master this one! Be careful because it's harder than it looks. Be sure and look at the correct answers afterward, so you can do better next time.
http://www.times.st-pete.fl.us/Egypt/Quiz/EgyptQuiz.html
Melissa Edwards, 14

King Tut-Anhk-Amun

Did you know that King Tutankhamen...? How do I know? I visited the King Tutankhamun Web site! It's got the coolest picture of King Tut's sarcophagus! This site has tons of interesting information about King Tut, but the text isn't written in an interesting way. Nonetheless, the site gets the facts out straight! King Tut's Web site is great for school reports. If you want to learn some cool facts about King Tut, this is the place for you!
http://www.geocities.com/TheTropics/2815/tut.html
Morgan Balavage, 12

Egyptian Gods

This site is most definitely a research center. It's full of information about early Egyptians and the gods they believed in. It has tons of information with more than fifty gods listed.
http://www.contrib.andrew.cmu.edu/~shawn/egypt//gods.html
Kellie Vaughn, 13

Tut's Curse

"Death shall come on swift wings to him that toucheth the tomb of Pharaoh." So reads a totally imaginary inscription supposedly in the tomb of Tutankhamun. On April 5, 1923, six weeks after opening the burial chamber of Tutankhamun's tomb, Lord Carnarvon, who had financed the excavations, died from complications resulting from a mosquito bite, and for years afterward, the death of anyone connected with the discovery of the tomb was attributed by the media to the Mummy's Curse.
Encyclopedia Smithsonian
http://www.si.edu/welcome/faq/pyramid.htm

Myths & Legends

For years people have made up myths to explain themselves, and that's how mythology was born. At least that's our story

Folklore & Mythology Electronic Texts

This page has a long list of folktales, myths, legends, and other stories from all over the world, that will be enjoyed by everyone who takes the time to read them. Once you get started, you'll find it hard to stop, as you read through the many great choices listed here.
http://www.pitt.edu/~dash/folktexts.html
Melissa Edwards, 14

Q: What Roman God is the month of January named after?

A: Janus, the God of doors, beginnings, and endings.
http://www.intergate.net /uhtml/.jhunt/greek_myth /janus.html

Princeton Classical Mythology HQ

If you enjoy mythology, or need the information for home-work, you should be able to find what you want from this site. From this page you can access all the pages related to classical mythology at Princeton University. Some of the site's features include a map of ancient Greece, and many other, more detailed regional maps, as well as sections on women in classical mythology. This page is expanding all the time.
http://www.princeton.edu/~markwoon/Myth
Philip Reilly, 12

Irish Mythology

This page has everything you could ever want to know about Irish mythology. It is a very plain page, which might put you off at first, but beneath this boring exterior you may find something interesting. It contains all sorts of stories which express the beliefs and history of the early Celts. This is very much a special-interest site.

http://www.paddynet.ie/island/newgrange/mythology.html
Philip Reilly, 12

Norse Mythology

This page gives you a look at all of the things that have to do with Norse mythology. It has a list of all of the Norse gods and goddesses, including their appropriate myths. It tells how the universe was formed according to Norse myths, and it gives lots and lots of interesting information on other Norse myths.

http://www.ugcs.caltech.edu/~cherryne/mythology.html
Andrea Bonilla, 13

Myths and Legends

Here is another site containing an extensive list of links to myths, folktales, and legends from all over the world. Divided by categories, you can very easily find what you are looking for. This site can be used for research purposes or just for fun.

http://pubpages.unh.edu/~cbsiren/myth.html
Melissa Edwards, 14

The Underground People

COOL KID SITE

Ancient Irish mythology tells the story of the Tuatha D'e Danaan, a divine people who came from the West and settled in Ireland. They were magical people, who could cause the moon to eclipse for three days, among other things. After their defeat by the Gaelic people, the predecessors of the modern Irish, an agreement was reached between the Tuatha D'e Danaan and the Gaels: They would share the country. The Gaels would live above the ground, the Tuatha D'e Danaan below.

Mythology
http://www.paddynet.ie /island/newgrange /mythology.html

The Round Table

There was a time when people believed a spell could turn a person into all kinds of things, and that winning a fight proved God was on your side. It was the age of King Arthur

An Arthurian Film List

This is a list of movies that are related in any way to the Arthurian period. The films date back prior to 1940 and as recent as the 1990s. The year each movie was made and a short description are included.
http://reality.sgi.com/employees/chris_manchester
/filmlist.html
Melissa Edwards, 14

Ian's Land of Castles

If you like castles or want to know more about them, visit this site! Ian is only 8 years old but he did a lot of research to make this great page! It tells about the inside and outside of castles and lots more, like how people in castles defended themselves in medieval times. One thing they sometimes did was to throw dead cows from the roof of the castles to spread disease among their enemies! If you want to know more, you HAVE to visit this page!
http://www.darling.hhdev.psu.edu/castles.htm#top
David Sawchak, 7

Arthurian FAQ

This is a nice page. It has a lot of writing, but it contains a lot of information on the medieval era. It answers questions such as: Who was Arthur? What was Camelot? How many knights of the Round Table were there? What books should I read to learn about it? and Where can I send to get a copy of a movie?
http://reality.sgi.com/employees/chris_manchester/faq.html
Emily Malloch, 11

The Castles of Wales

Wales, a.k.a. The Land of Castles, is "home of some of the world's most outstanding examples of medieval castle-building." Tour these castles through awesome photos, and find out about the peoples who built these wonders of architecture and why. There are more than 100 images to choose from, so if you like castles and kings and all that stuff, be prepared to spend some time here.
http://www.wp.com/castlewales/home.html
Nykki-Lynn Smelser, 10

Camelot!

Some people believe that Cadbury castle, in Somerset, is the one that many Arthurian legends refer to as Camelot. Historians know that it was occupied in Arthurian times by a powerful leader and many followers, but that's about the sum of the evidence. Fortunately, there are enough pictures on the Web of British castles that survive today to give you a glimpse into the living conditions of medieval times.

Castles on the Web
http://fox.nstn.ca/~tmonk /castle/castle.html

COOL KID SITE

Holidays

Can't wait for your next holiday? Well, the Web is a great place to help you pass the time until the next Big Event, and you might find a holiday you hadn't heard of!

Mother's Day on the Net

This is the perfect site to visit as a family. This tribute to Mom is filled with cute animations, a video, activities, poems, and more. Read about the history of Mother's Day and learn a great way to celebrate it, as background music plays while you browse. It's all here at Mother's Day on the Net!
http://www.melizo.com/holidays/mother
Melissa Edwards, 14

KWANZAA

During the week of Kwanzaa, which was founded in 1966 by Dr. Maulana Karenga, many African Americans gather in the evenings to celebrate "the oneness and goodness of life."
Kwanzaa Information Center
http://www.melanet.com
/melanet/kwanzaa
/kwanzaa.html

Season's Greetings

This is a cool site, especially the link that tells you how many months, days, hours, minutes and seconds 'til Christmas (updated every 12 seconds! but HOW?). There are also links to pages where you can learn about how other cultures celebrate Christmas, learn how to say "Merry Christmas" in 33 languages, or learn about Santa's new MH 2600 Cyber-Sleigh (VERRY fast!).
http://christmas.com
David Sawchak, 7

The First Thanksgiving

Read this article to learn the "real truth" about the Thanksgiving holiday. You'll find links to things such as the Mayflower II, the 1627 Pilgrim Village, and recipes for foods at the great feast. You can even read a first-hand account by a leader of the pilgrim colony, Edward Winslow.
http://media3.com/plymouth/thanksgiving.htm
Melissa Edwards, 14

Hanukkah

Happy Hanukkah! This fun page is all about the Jewish holiday. You can learn what exactly Hanukkah is, read the Hanukkah story, and even make potato latkes from their recipe! And why not download part of the Dreidl Song? There are links to a Christmas page and a Kwanzaa page, too. So, Hag Sameach! (Happy Holiday!)
http://www.harpercollins.com/kids/hanu.htm
Carol Scott, 13

Groundhog Day

On this site there are heaps of pics and lots of info on Groundhog Day. If you are into clubs, there is a club you can join for $7.50 and you get a card, newsletter and weather prognostication. You can also get special deals if your birthday falls on "HOG DAY." If you happen to get bored you can play a game or read the predictions from 1880 until now.
http://www.groundhog.org
Rachel Prior, 11

Q: Who was St. Valentine and how did he die?

A: He married young couples and he was beheaded.
The Valentine's Day Game
http://www.stern.nyu.edu/Valentine

True or False: St. Patrick was Irish.

False. He was British.
A Wee Bit O' Fun
http://www1.nando.net/toys/stpaddy/stpaddy.html

Do you want to find a holiday for practically every day of the year? Try this out!
Festival & Holiday Chart
http://www.hooked.net/users/twerp23/festchartchart.html

HOLIDAYS
The 4th

Location : http://www.westcomm.com/lib-comm/libe

Netsite : http://www.thing.net/~janine/firework.gif

Location : http://grid.let.rug.nl/~welling/usa/images/decindependence.gif

# of July

In CONGRESS, JULY 4, 1776.

The unanimous Declaration of the thirteen united States of America,

Declaring Independence

All of you history buffs who like to surf the Net should visit this place. It has lots of info on the Declaration of Independence, as well as related documents and pictures. You should remember this place the next time you need to do some research for a history project.

http://lcweb.loc.gov/exhibits/declara/declara1.html

Katie Tandler, 13

Vikings

Ah, Vikings! Raiding and pillaging was their game. They were rather good at it. But they were also traders, explorers, and settlers, leaving their mark wherever they went

The Viking Home Page

This Viking Home Page is not only a great place to study but also to have fun! It tells about the Vikings throughout their age, 793–1066 A.D. It tells you what they ate and drank and it also shows the structure of their very cool ships. But that's not all—you can see pictures of Viking runes and see how all sorts of things were made.

http://www.control.chalmers.se/vikings/viking.html

Elizabeth Wolff, 12

Jorvik Viking Centre

Have you ever wanted to travel through time and see an ancient town in action? This site informs you about the next best thing: the Jorvik Viking Centre in York, England. You can learn about what Vikings did during everyday life. Pretty soon, there will be sound files available for downloading, but until then, you can still enjoy the descriptive text that makes you feel as if you were right there in the midst of the action.

http://www.demon.co.uk/tourism/jvc

Katie Tandler, 13

Viking Heritage

Here you can read a little bit about the Vikings and take a quiz to test how much you know about them. If you choose the right answer they even have a picture to explain it for you. You can go to Viking links also and go to other places that give you lots of information on Vikings.
http://bull.got.kth.se/~viking/index.html
Alexandra Barsk, 12

Vikings!

This is the superior place to learn about Vikings. It has lots of serious info while it also has funny stuff, like Vikings didn't really wear horns! There are loads of graphics and even a guide to Viking footwear! The only thing that is annoying is that it is so huge you can easily get a little lost. Take your time and you will find a lot of fun material.
http://www.n-vision.com/spoon/vikes/index.html
Rachel Prior, 11

GET THIS!

Wrestling was such an important part of Viking life that wrestling rules were part of their laws!

The Vikings loved sports and games. Their favorites were wrestling, archery, javelin, skiing, swimming, knattleikr (their version of baseball), backgammon, nine man's morris, and fox and geese.

Leif Ericson was the first European known to have discovered and settled on this continent in 1003 A.D., nearly 500 years before Columbus.
The Viking Network
http://odin.nls.no/viking

The Wild West

The heroes of the West weren't invented by the movies. Jesse James, Billy the Kid, and the rest were the biggest stars of their day

National Cowboy Hall of Fame

Here you can learn all about the National Cowboy Hall of Fame. Learn about the founder, its history and the fun and interesting things to see and do. Hours, admission fees, and information on how to contact the National Cowboy Hall of Fame are also included at this site.
http://www.netplus.net/okc/cowboy.html

Calamity Jane

This is the autobiography of Martha Cannary Burke, also known as "Calamity Jane." You can read this interesting story of her life in three parts. Part One deals with her childhood, growing up outdoors, and becoming known as "Calamity Jane." Part Two talks about her friendship with Wild Bill Hickok and their adventures together. In Part Three, she tells about her family life, becoming a wife and a mother. This is an interesting story that will be enjoyed by all who take the time to read it.
http://www.eskimo.com/~chorus/jane/index.html

Buffalo Bill

Here's a site filled with all the information one would ever need about William F. Cody, better known as "Buffalo Bill." There's even a timeline that ranges from 1846 to 1986. Still not satisfied? Check out the Suggested Readings list to see other places where you can find information on this historic legend.
ftp://ftp.wave.park.wy.us/pub/cody/chamber/codybio.txt

Billy the Kid Outlaw Gang

Billy the Kid Outlaw Gang is an organization that is designed to "preserve, protect, and promote Billy the Kid/Pat Garrett history in New Mexico." This site gives information on the club and how to become a member.
http://www.nmia.com/~btkog

CowboyPals

CowboyPals is a site mainly for those interested in the old Western movies and TV shows. If you're a fan of Roy Rogers and Trigger, Gene Autry, or Hopalong Cassidy, be sure to check this place out. There are sound and movie clips, lots of pictures, and a neat background.
http://www.cowboypal.com
All Wild West reviews by Melissa Edwards, 14

COOL KID SITE

Was Billy the Kid Bad When He Really Was a Kid?

One friend of Billy the Kid remembered him later:

"He was kind and could be a good friend, but I am sure we should not make a hero of Billy, for after all he was a bandit and a killer."

Interview withLittle Berta Ballard, http://lcweb2.loc.gov /ammem/ammemhome.html

i find the Internet very useful for my homework and research. There are plenty of sites to help you find the information you need. There are also things like Barbie pages for girls. If you're a boy, you may prefer computer game pages where you can download games, and learn a few tricks! You can also create your own personal page through several pages like Angelfire.com! What else could a kid want? But I'm not saying the Internet is perfect. There are some server errors which you get now and then and also lots of junk mail!

Derya
Davenport 11
ANKARA, TURKEY

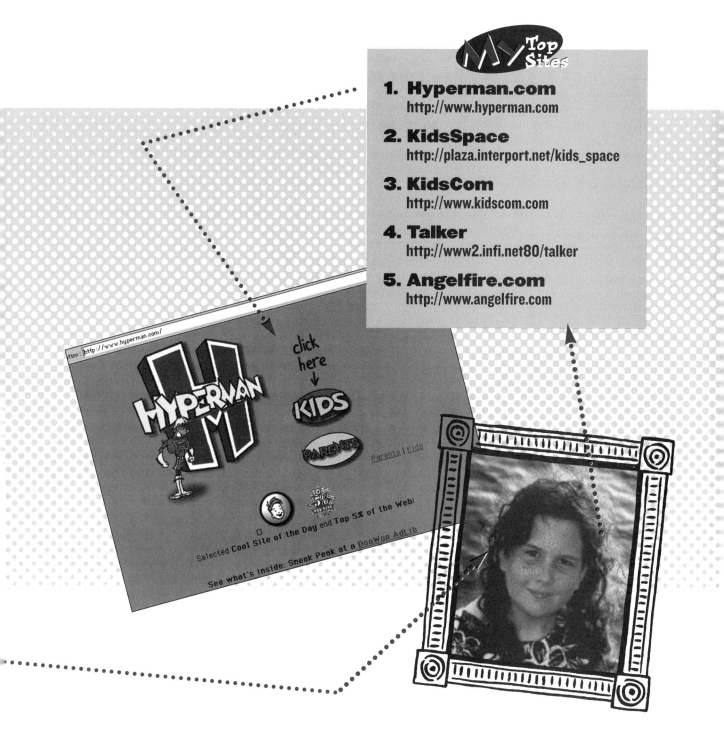

My Top Sites

1. **Hyperman.com**
   http://www.hyperman.com

2. **KidsSpace**
   http://plaza.interport.net/kids_space

3. **KidsCom**
   http://www.kidscom.com

4. **Talker**
   http://www2.infi.net80/talker

5. **Angelfire.com**
   http://www.angelfire.com

Star Info

You've never met them, but you feel that you know them. And why not? You've shared many adventures on the screen—now meet them online

Hollywood Online

Whether you are searching for a new movie to see this weekend, or you'd just like to follow up on that hot new actor or actress, check out this terrific site. To start with, there are wonderful back-grounds of eye-catching color. If you would like to take a stroll through the gift shop, then simply click on the icon and head straight for your favorite movie or TV show's page, packed full of memorabilia for every fan in the house. If shopping isn't on your mind, how about trying one of the four new chat lines? There's a wonderful channel just waiting for you to "sign-on." However, for those of you without a Global Chat networking system, you can download one for free. Although it does take a while for the full download-ing process to end.
http://www.hollywood.com
Kellie Vaughn, 13

The Movie Sounds Page

Bookmark this site! They have all your favorite sounds from lots of your favorite movies that you can listen to with Real Audio or download

as a .WAV file. They even have all of the programs you need to listen to and play with your sounds. While you're there, see if you can figure out the Mystery Sound. There are also links to other sound pages.
http://www.moviesounds .com
Kelsey Mays, 11

Michele's Celebrity Homepage

This site is impressive, it's well-designed, and has lots of graphics which are pretty cool. However, it tends to go off the topic of celebrities and talk about clubs and other stuff, and the information on celebrities is only O.K. And you can only find out about one celebrity an issue unless you write to Michele.
http://www.geocities.com /Hollywood/4823
Bronwyn Lee, 12

Directory of Sandra Bullock Net Resources

This site has to be the best Sandra Bullock site on the Web. No person, young or old, could pass this site by. The site has many great links including general information on and about Sandra Annette Bullock, terrific still images, her current film information, and recent interviews. Check this site out for your viewing delight! One problem: This site isn't updated often, but you could write to her manager at the address listed at the bottom of the page to get the updated scoop.
http://www .eecs.wsu.edu /~tmenagh /sabfc
Kellie Vaughn, 13

Tom Cruise Homepage

A haven of pics, articles, and info about Tom's films, including facts, quotes, sounds, links, and biography. A fan-run home page that has all the info needed for any fan. Simple, yet effective. Very good, with lots of pages.
http://www.cyberhighway.net /~phlacin/cruise.html
Hayley Morgan, 12

Location: http://user.aol.com/agnttexmex/images/sandra-b.jpg

Penn & Teller FAQ

This site is a list of frequently asked questions about Penn & Teller. It includes a tour schedule, and an answer to just about every question you could ask about Penn & Teller. Although the questions are arranged by categories, it still may take a little bit of scrolling to find the question you want.
http://ai.eecs.umich.edu /people/nielsen/alt.fan .penn-n-teller-faq
Leslie Safier, 12

Stills from River's Movies

This site is good, but only if you wanted to check out a couple of still poses of River Phoenix himself. This site only contains photos from four of his movies, and doesn't house any other useful information. So, unless you have all the information, and just wanted something to remember him by, look here.
http://www.science .uwaterloo.ca/~ma3reid /rivmov.html
Kellie Vaughn, 13

The Society for Keanu Consciousness

This site is an online shrine to actor Keanu Reeves. As the creator of this page put it:
"We at the Society for Keanu Consciousness believe that the block- buster actor Keanu Reeves is in fact this century's premier avatar of divinity and peace!" If you like Keanu, and if you agree with these guys (or even if you don't), you should visit this place. It has lots of pics, sound files taken from (where else?) his movies, and a whole bunch more. Very nice, and extremely funny.
http://www.empirenet.com /~jahvah/skc/skc.html
Katie Tandler, 13

of a show and other places where you never dreamed your favorite actress would be—even places you have been! The site has no hard-to-understand parts! It's Winona's best site! **http://www.dvc.auburn.edu/~harshec/www/Winona.html**
Jillian Tellez, 9

You can vote how many stars you would like to give the film. Besides the ratings, you can also see credits to the film or follow links to see reviews, locations. This page will not give you a summary of the movies or a very good biography on Robin Williams, however. **http://us.imdb.com/M/person-exact?+williams%2C+robin**
Leslie Safier, 12

The Winona Ryder Site

This is the best site for Winona Ryder! You can see pictures, get info, get her TV schedule, go behind the scenes, find out why people think she's the best actress and lots, lots more! There are no parts that aren't interesting for people who really like Winona. The best part is that you can see pictures of Winona on covers of magazines, at home, in the middle

Robin Williams Filmography

This is a list of films Robin Williams has been in. This gives a short biography of Robin Williams. The films are rated by people's votes.

THE TEMPLE OF Jim Carrey

This is an imaginative and well-presented site. There are some pretty good graphics and heaps of links to photos from Jim's movies, or movies Jim has appeared in. It's quite a nice site, and pleasing to the eye, but there's no info on him whatsoever.

http://pages.prodigy.com/jcarrey

Hayley Morgan, 12

"ALLLRiiGHHHTYYYY THEN!!"

Favorite Shows & Movies

Whether it's a program you love or a program you love to hate, or a movie you can't forget, you can find out everything you want to know about it online

ABC

The ABC Home Page is based entirely on ABC, the television network. Filled with cool graphics, the ABC home page has lots of unique features, like the daily news scrolling across the bottom of the screen, the top stories, the weather forecast, and everything else you would expect to see on the news. This site is excellent if you have Real Audio! If you're interested in computers, there's even a computer section. This is a great site to visit on the Internet.
http://www.abctelevision.com
David Lindsay, 11

Netsite: http://abc.com/primetime/html/days/fri/friframe.html

ABC Primetime — BOY meets WORLD
THE ABC TELEVISION NETWORK

video & audio PREVIEW

Oct 11. (9:30/8:30 Central)

"Fishing For Virna" - Cory's new-found appreciation for the meaning of family prompts him to help reunite a hopeful Shawn with his mother, Virna, who comes back to town after searching for a better life. Also, Cory, explores ways to honor the memory of Brenda, the beloved and

CTW Family Corner

This site is the official Children's Television Workshop home page. It has lots of related information, including games for kids and parenting info. The games are geared toward preschool-age kids, with everything from dress-up games to alphabet-coloring games. There is also an entertainment listing for preschoolers on this site.
http://www.ctw.org
Erin Fleege, 13

Fox

This page is all about Fox, the broadcasting company. The Fox Web site includes three different sections: Fox Kids, Fox Entertainment, and Fox Sports. The best part of Fox Kids is the Fox Kids Countdown. It tells all about the Countdown, and you can even vote on your favorite songs! On Fox Entertainment, the coolest part is the Fox Fun House. In it, you can download lots of cool stuff, and also send a friend a Fox email postcard! The Fox Sports site has a lot of articles about sports events. The most fun part of this site is the baseball quiz! The Fox Web site is very interesting and includes a lot of fun stuff. Everyone should enjoy this site!

http://www.foxnetwork.com
Erin Fleege, 13

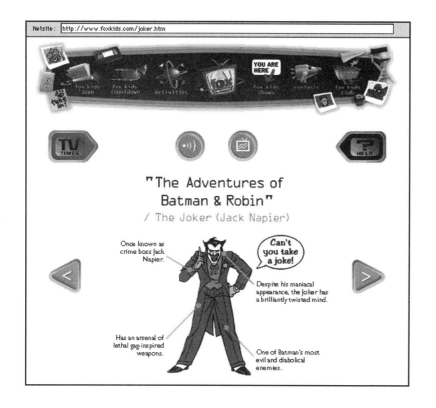

Netsite: http://www.foxkids.com/joker.htm

"The Adventures of Batman & Robin"
/ The Joker (Jack Napier)

Once known as crime boss Jack Napier.

Can't you take a joke!

Despite his maniacal appearance, the Joker has a brilliantly twisted mind.

Has an arsenal of lethal gag-inspired weapons.

One of Batman's most evil and diabolical enemies.

TV Theme Songs & More

A good selection of TV theme tunes and songs. Mostly children's programs, but there are a few of all sorts! (Including a few strange ones, like *The Simpstones?!* Is that a mix of *The Simpsons* and *The Flintstones?*) This is a well-presented site, with great graphics, making it easier to access. The sounds are of good quality and this is heaven for anyone with sound. It's a great place to visit. Make sure you pop by with all ears open, and you'll soon be humming along to all of those groovy theme tunes,

even *The Smurfs*!
http://wso.williams.edu /~mgarland/sounds
Hayley Morgan, 12

Deep Web Nine

Calling all *Star Trek* fans... this is a MUST see! Get ready to transport around the winner of at least two awards for best *Star Trek* site... a place where you can find information on every *Star Trek* episode aired (whether the original *Star Trek, Deep Space Nine,* etc.) plus *Babylon 5* and all the *Star Wars* movies, and other sci-fi stuff. To find out all the other things you will discover here, you've got to beam down... you won't be disappointed.
http://www.tut.fi/~pekka
Nykki-Lynn Smelser, 10

Disney Villains

From Ursula the Sea Witch to Mozenrath from the *Aladdin* series, this is one of the most sinister Web sites around. Disney Villains starts with that famous Disney logo. At first, it's boring because it's still "under construction." Villains that reside here now include Pete, the Evil Queen/Witch from *Snow White*, Mozenrath, and Ursula the Sea Witch. Click on one of them and see the picture and read some information about them. The pictures and text are very impressive and show the diligence and hard work it takes to put each villain together.
http://www.erinet.com /nitebrdr/villains.html
Morgan Balavage, 12

The Gargoyles Homepage

A really enjoyable page with all the action and excitement of the TV show. It contains all sorts of info about the show. All-Star Line-up is a page about all the guest stars and what episodes they appear in. The Fun and Games section includes trivia, a coloring book page and a word search puzzle. The best parts are the movies, which show clips from the best bits from the show. Definitely a page that will keep you occupied and entertained.
http://www.tvplex.com /TVplex/BuenaVista /Gargoyles
Philip Reilly, 12

©Buena Vista Television

Official MCA Hercules Home Page

Relax or tremble within the mythical world of a half man/half god. Television's hero, Hercules, will entertain and amuse you. Meet the cast and production team, check the TV schedules, and read a magazine while listening to music. Join in the chat forum. Try your luck with the Beast Master Competition.
http://www.mca.com/tv /hercules
Rachel Prior, 11

Welcome to Jumanji

What a superb movie site! One of the very best on the Web, with excellent graphics and wonderful information! You can learn about the movie and its characters, the cast, the crew, filming, etc. This site gives you a behind-the-scenes look at the movie, as well as a chance to play the Jumanji game. This site is imaginative, creative, and original. Quite a trip for anyone on the Web!
http://www.spe.sony .com/Pictures/Sony Movies/Jumanji
Hayley Morgan, 12

Mad About You

Here's the best *Mad About You* page on the Internet. It's filled with cool stuff. First, you'll want to take a look at the photos and watch the video clip of the hilarious cast. Then, you have to hear the audio clips. Learn all about the stars of the comedy, Paul Reiser and Helen Hunt, plus get links to all your other favorite TV shows like *The Nanny* and *Seinfeld*.
http://www.spe.sony.com /Pictures/tv/mad/mad.html
Melissa Edwards, 14

Netsite: http://www.spe.sony.com/Pictures/tv/mad/assets/c1f1.jpg

Melrose Place

Anyone who watches *Melrose Place* is sure to have a good time visiting this site. Get the scoop on what's going on with the stars, and read a note from Amanda. Take a look inside the basement, where you'll get all the hottest news and gossip. There's even a chat room! Stuff changes all the time here, so if you don't come back often, you'll miss something good.
http://melroseplace.com
Melissa Edwards, 14

The Morphing Grid (Power Rangers)

GO, GO POWER RANGERS!!! If you are a Power Rangers fan you just CAN'T miss this! For "hot," just-off-the-press info (before it even gets to your TV), check this site. This site is run BY a Power Rangers fan and is FOR all Power Rangers fans (kids and adults who are still kids-at-heart). Here, along with information about EVERYTHING in Power Ranger history since the first season, you can find Fan Art, Fan Fiction and lots, Lots, LOTS more!!!! Fans even have the chance to become Web Rangers and create their own Web Ranger home page. To become a Web Ranger you must first find The Web Crystal. Click The Web Crystal for further instructions. (PSST! For all of you that are DYING to find The Web Crystal, click on Monster Gallery and go down to the bottom. YOU CAN'T MISS IT!)
http://ic.www.media.mit.edu /Personal/manny/power
David Sawchak, 7

Muppets & Stuff

This Muppets site is very large and has a lot of good information "and stuff!" If you're interested in the Muppets, take a look. Along with the Episode Guide, Fast-Food Guide, Lyrics Page, and more, there is also a large links section to many more Muppets sites, and more links to other sorts of

sites. No, this isn't the official Muppets site, but it's getting pretty close to it!

http://www.megalink.net /~cooke

Erin Fleege, 13

Julie's Party of Five

This site was nice but too old for me, more of a teenage site. I saw lots of pictures of the stars and cool clapperboard icons for links to other pages. You can get all the info on this show here, but it isn't real interesting if you don't watch the show. I Lost interest after five minutes

because there was too much reading. I don't know this TV show so I didn't stay long but I think it would be a fun site if you were a fan, but who has time for TV anymore, with the Web to check out?

http://www.txdirect.net /users/julie/party.html

Amy Schroeder, 10

Ren 'n' Stimpy Page

If you want to know when, where, and why you should watch *The Ren 'n' Stimpy Show*, go and check out this page! Go to the FAQ section to find out some of the most common questions you could ask, like how do you pronounce Ren's name? Then take a peek at the unofficial episode list, where you can

finale. The monologs (Seinfeld's stand up comedy) are fun to read through if you need a good laugh. There are about 10 or so of them. And the character bios include a picture of each character. On the quotes page, you can read everyone else's favorite *Seinfeld* quotes, and then submit your own. This site was obviously created by a devoted *Seinfeld* fan!
http://greg.simplenet.com /seinfeld
Erin Fleege, 13

3-D Homer and The Simpsons

This page is OK. The graphics of 3-D Homer are neat, but how come only ONE of the pictures worked? Well, besides that it was OK. It had a list of everything Bart had ever written on the chalkboard. That was kind of neat. The info on each

check to see if you are watching a repeat or just read about the shows! And if you haven't had enough, view the Ren 'n' Stimpy links page where you will find cool links to other people's sites.
http://www.lysator.liu.se /~marcus/ren_stimpy
Joe Conrad, 13

Seinfeld Online

If you like *Seinfeld*, be sure to check out this site. Some of the things included in Seinfeld Online are short character bios, Seinfeld monologs, show synopses, and quotes. You can also read other *Seinfeld* watchers' comments about the season

Location: http://www.best.com/~jnc/simp/images/upcoming

episode got a little boring. *The Simpsons* is such a cool show it needs a cool page.
http://www.mit.edu:800l /people/cwward/TheSimpsons .html
Emily Malloch, 11

Space Ghost's Ghost Planet

For all you Space Ghost fans, check out his spot. Find your way through the Super Secret Mine Shaft, tour Moltar's Lava Pit (his bedroom, control room, and other rooms in his futuristic pad), visit Zorak's Locus Club, and stop by the Quick Stoppe shops. Younger kids will probably enjoy this site more than the teenagers.
http://www.ghost planet.com
Nykki-Lynn Smelser, 10

Some Tiny Toons Links

This page take you to a lyrics page for all the *Tiny Toons* songs and to other pages with really nice pictures of all the characters. The best thing about *Tiny Toons* is that there are lots of girls characters, like Babs Bunny. They're funnier than the *Loony Toons*, too.
http://ally.ios.com /~eggiel9/TTA.html
Susanna Wolff, 8

X-Files: Operation Paperclip

A stylish Web site which has everything for the keen X-Phile. *X-Files* Judgment Day includes FAQs, pictures, sounds, movies, episode guides, lots of links, chat news and mail. If that's not enough, you could take a peek at the X-Vault, which is full of news articles, books, and comics. And if you want to join a fan club, there's one on this site. You could become an official X-Phile. A really good site. Well worth a visit.
http://www.powerup.com.au /~tcook/xfiles.html
Philip Reilly, 12

Location: http://www.geocities.com/Hollywood/7452/phone.jpg

Teen Movie
CRITIC

Hey kids! Here's your chance to get the scoop on the latest movies out there from another kid... well, a teenager. The rating system goes from one star, meaning "bad, don't watch," to four stars, meaning "excellent, must see." A new film is reviewed every day! There's also a special section called "Director of the Week" that lets you learn about the famous director's life and work. This site deserves a thumbs up!

**http://www.dreamagic.com/roger
/teencritic.html**

Melissa Edwards, 14

Location: http://www2.stargalaxy.com/img_orig/IG/0/4/6/mc28

Location: http://www.spe.sony.com/Pictures/SonyMovies/movies/Matilda/

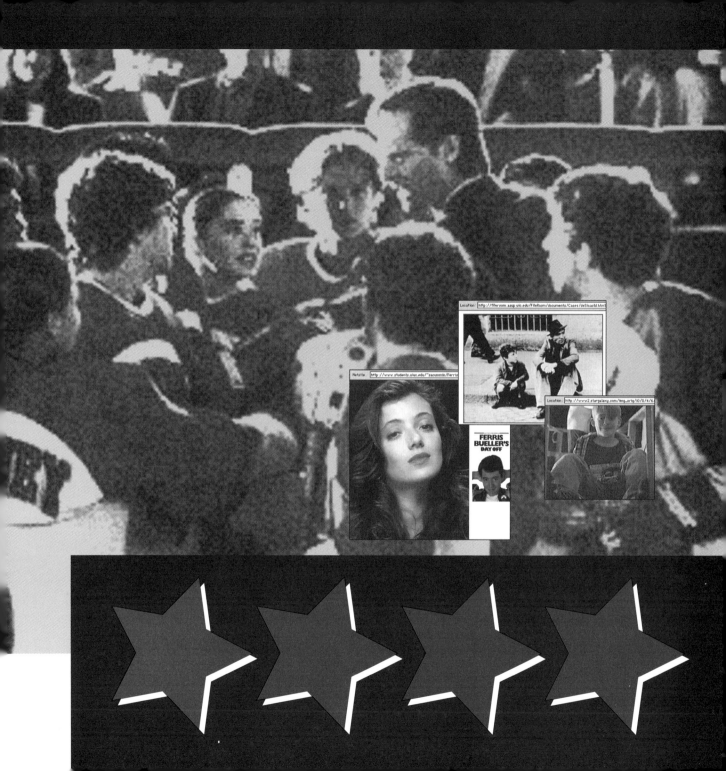

Location : http://fileroom.aaup.uic.edu/FileRoom/documents/Cases/deSicaold.html

Netsite : http://www.students.uiuc.edu/~saoummin/Ferris

Location : http://www2.stargalaxy.com/img_orig/10/0/4/6.

FERRIS
BUELLER'S
DAY OFF

Music Artists

Take a walk on the Web side with your favorite groups and artists. Here you'll find videos, soundclips, pictures, and more

The Ultimate Band List

This is a HUGE list! I wouldn't be surprised if a million bands were listed! Most of the bands that are listed you've probably never heard of. The best thing about the list is that it's nicely organized and has its own search engine. This site has it all, from ALL 4 ONE to ZZ Top. This list is a MUST-SEE! It even has great graphics to further add to your enjoyment.
http://www.ubi.com
Jeff Little, 13

Eyeneer Music Archives (jazz, contemporary classical, international and American music)

On this site there are six types of archive, all great in their own way. There are International and American music archives, Contemporary Classical, New Jazz, and the Definitive Eyeneer archive. Each of these has loads of great stuff. They all have biographies and discographies of musicians, new releases, photos, and even Quicktime movies and sound samples. This site also has the latest on record labels and some good pictures.
http://www.eyeneer.com
David Reilly, 10

Harmony Central

Harmony Central is an internet resource for musicians. You can read FAQs about instruments. You can download shareware. There are many music-related links. You can also buy or sell an instrument through ads. You can even get your own music on the internet. This is a great place for music lovers!
http://www.harmony -central.com
Leslie Safier, 12

Gary's Tori Amos

This Tori Amos tribute was made by one of her biggest fans. He gives links to many of the best Tori pages on the Net and has stuff relating to her music, lyrics, interviews, and photos. He's got a very cool background. Check it out!
http://web.cal.msu.edu/gary /tori.html
Melissa Edwards, 14

Tori Amos Premiere

This site is the official Tori Amos site. Here you will find a lot of stuff on Tori, as well as her albums. The best part of the site right now is the Q&A section. Here, you will find out about Tori straight from her own mouth. If you're a Tori Amos fan, check out Tori.com!
http://www.tori.com
Erin Fleege, 13

Mike's Beatles Page

This has lots of information and pictures on the Beatles. Its contents include a huge variety of things like a picture gallery, news, musical things, and stuff about all four members of the band. This is a really good place to go if you are a fan of the Beatles or if you just want to look at some pictures of this popular music group.
http://www.eecis.udel.edu /~markowsk/beatles
Alexandra Barsk, 12

Toppermost of the Poppermost

This Web site is filled with TONS of stuff on the Beatles. It links you to almost every site on the subject of the "Lads from Liverpool." You can see album covers and a really beautiful picture of John. You can read the lyrics to Beatles songs or read the 101 reasons to be a Beatles fan. These are only a few of the many things that you can do at this site.
http://www.umd.umich.edu /~infinit/Beatles
Alexandra Barsk, 12

All About Boyz II Men

This Boyz II Men site is definitely one of the best on the Web. Here, you can find tons of stuff, from a discography and videography, to lyrics and the band members' personal information. You can also download a .WAV file of Boyz II Men introducing themselves. This site is unique, because it's the very first homepage devoted specifically to Boyz II Men. If you're looking for info on Boyz II Men, here's where to look.
http://www.cyber-dyne.com /~Jenh
Erin Fleege, 13

Dreamworld

This Web site is incredibly fascinating! Even though it doesn't have any Mariah Carey songs that you can listen to, you will find lyrics to two or three songs from every album she made. You can also read cool facts about how she created her songs and neat facts about her life. This Web site displays beautiful pictures of Mariah Carey. Although some points of this site might be a bore, there are some really fun things to read and do!
http://superchannel.pair.com /Dreamworld
Elizabeth Wolff, 12

Greenday.com

If you like Green Day, this is a fab Web site. It has lists of articles on Green Day you can read, video clips and pictures you can download,

Location: http://www.greenday.com/

album info and the words to some Green Day songs. The webmasters say they're organizing some kind of chat with Green Day, but those things usually take a lot of time. A great Web site! Even if you don't like Green Day, this is a fun place to check out.
http://www.greenday.com
Samantha Lipton, 12

The Official Hootie and the Blowfish WebSite

This is a pretty cool Web site. It has lots of stuff about the band. You can get to this information by going to six different topics including Band Bios, Tour Dates, and Lyrics. There are also two other topics under which you can purchase Hootie and the Blowfish merchandise or email the band. This is a great place to go if you are a Hootie and the Blowfish fan.
http://www.hootie.com /hootie.html
Alexandra Barsk, 12

Go On Girl... Miss Janet!!!

Lots of Janet pictures. Great if you were already a Janet fan. Not so great if you wanted to know more about her. The webmaster should show pictures of her from more than one or two videos. There should be some trivia questions for those who want to test their Janet Jackson knowledge.
http://www.opendoor.com /WeRemember/jdj.html
Tweba Sargeant, 12

Location: http://www.opendoor.com/WeRemember/janet_125th_St.GIF

Led Zeppelin Archive

If you are a rock fan, this is your "Stairway to Heaven!" This page provides you with images, links to other pages, lyrics, and Digital Graffiti (Led Zeppelin Mailing List) of Led Zeppelin! One tiny thing that makes this page a little dull is that it doesn't have a background. Other than that this page may be small, but it is okay.

http://www.jbrowne.com /Zeppelin/zeppelin.html

Alex Landback, 10

Location: http://server.mediasoft.net/thomasme/

Madonna: On the Net

This site has lots of news about Madonna but not enough stuff about Madonna herself. In some parts it gets a little boring but for most of it shows wonderful pictures and is very fun and interesting.

http://www.geocities.com/ Hollywood/2837

Susanna Wolff, 8

Cyber Alanis

This Web site is the best if you want lots of fun information on Alanis. You can go to eight different topics including lyrics, pictures, articles, and sound. You can listen to parts of some of her songs under Sound or just read the lyrics if you go to Lyrics. If you want to see pictures of Alanis just click on Pictures and voila! There you have it! This site is extremely amusing and you're sure to have lotsa fun.

http://www.mediasoft.net /thomasme

Erin Fleege, 13

Oasis

Oasis is a great place for fans of the hot band Oasis. From tour dates to lyrics, this site is filled with tons of things. You can even email Oasis under Fan Mail! There is also information on an exclusive fan club. Furthermore, this site is terrific!

http://www.oasisinet.com
Kelly Roman, 11

TLC

This site is devoted to the music group TLC. It's a very well-done site, with lots of information and media. You can find a lot at this site, and if you don't, there are links to other sites, where you'll probably find what you are looking for. The best part is the collection of pictures, and there are about 20 to choose from. If you're a TLC fan, you should take a look at this site.

http://www.wku.edu /~pierccm/tlc
Erin Fleege, 13

U2 Magazine
The Zooropean

The Zoorapean is a magazine devoted to the band U2.

Inside this magazine you can find pictures, reviews of concerts, CDs and LPs, rare items, and much more. The cyberzine includes just some of the things in the real paper magazine. The magazine is issued four times a year, and so is the cyberzine. If you're into U2, check it out!

http://www.luna.nl/~u2zoorop
Erin Fleege, 13

MUSIC ARTISTS
MTV

The world's most popular music channel has a home page! Read the biographies of your favorite "video jockeys," or follow links to other music-related sites. Really awesome graphics along with very informative text make this page one of the best on the Internet.

http://www.mtv.com

Joe Conrad, 13

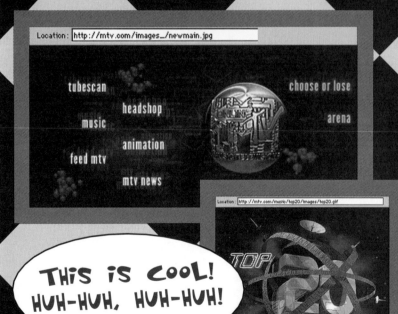

THIS IS COOL! HUH-HUH, HUH-HUH!

Location: http://mtv.com/music/buzz/images/buzzhome.gif

buzz clips

Location: http://mtv.com/tubescan/m2/images/banner.jpg

M2

Location: http://mtv.com/MTVNEWS/images/wirlogo.gif

WEEK IN ROCK

Location: http://www.mtv.com/music/bio/biodata/garbage

Garbage

Location: http://www.mtv.com/music/bio/biodat

Silverchair

Location: http://mtv.com/tubescan/rw5/

THE REAL WORLD V

BIOS
THIS WEEK'S SHOW
HOUSE TOUR
QUESTION OF THE WEEK

MIKE DAN
CYNTHIA JOE SARAH FLORA MELISSA

Seven Strangers.

QUESTION OF
What bothers you most a

Location: http://www.mtv.com/music/120min/images/onetwenty2.gif

120 MINUTES

Location: http://mtv.com/tubescan/vj/images/middle.gif

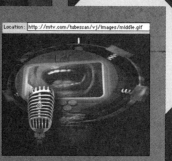

Superfriendly Sites

Can you say "Wha-am!", "BLADOO-OOM!", and "Karaka-taka-chow!"? And do you know what these words mean? If not, see below...

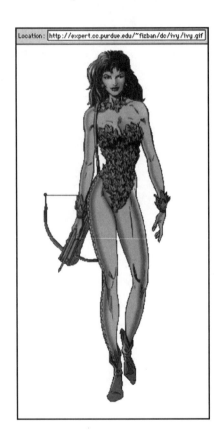

Location: http://expert.cc.purdue.edu/~fizban/dc/ivy/ivy.gif

Fitzbain's Guide to DC Comics

If your favorite comic book characters are DC Comic Book heroes, then bookmark this site! There is lots of information about all the best superheroes! There is more information and links available for the bigger and older characters, like Superman, than there is for the less popular ones like Wonder Woman. This was disappointing, but there is still enough to keep you busy for a long time!
http://expert.cc.purdue.edu /~fizban/dc/cd.html
Kelsey Mays, 11

DC Comics

DC Comics has a nice design and great graphics on their home page. Some of the different sections of the site are Nightwing, Digital trading cards, Sovereign Seven, Chomp, and The Final Night. Also, this site has the Superman Radio Special where you can listen to episodes of "Superman." It requires RealAudio. A must-see for comic lovers!
http://www.dccomics.com
Jeff Little, 13

The Bat Page

If you ever have to answer a trivia question about Batman,

Location: http://www.cire.com/batman/

go here. They answer lots of questions about Batman, Robin, and their friends and enemies. Did you know that Alfred used to be a short fat fellow and that his name was Alfred Beagle? You can send them a question if you don't already know the answer. There is also a Comic Collection Database program that you can download to help you keep track of your comic collection.

http://wchat.on.ca/web/bats /bats-b.htm
Kelsey Mays, 11

Mantle of the Bat

A must for all those Batman fans who watch the show on TV. The layout of this site is somewhat puzzling in parts, but no trouble for the dedicated Batman crusader. The Joker has his fair share of information and pictures. The picture gallery is not the best ever seen, but remains a worthwhile place to visit. The best segment is Movie News—do you know how far away the fourth Batman movie is?

http://www.cire.com/batman
Rachel Prior, 11

BatPage

Visit this page to learn all about the Caped Crusader and his friends and foes from the comic books. The thumb-

nail pictures lead to where you can find out the origins of your favorite characters, as well as bigger pics of them in action. This page is incredible!

http://www.tc.umn.edu /nlhome/g452/walk0043 /index.html
Katie Tandler, 13

Calvin and Hobbes Comic Gallery

If you still enjoy the fascination and delights of a picture comic book, this site should

Netsite: http://www.tc.umn.edu/nlhome/g452/walk0043/cat.html

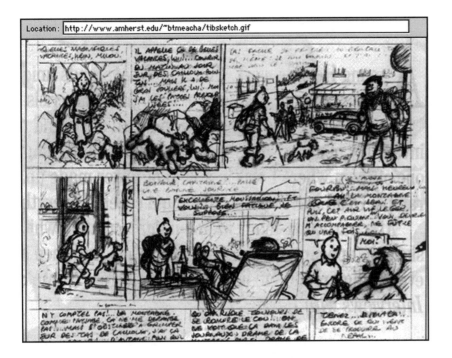

be bookmarked. Travel along with Calvin through his comic character world. Try your talent at creating a comic strip of your own. Plenty of bits and pieces you can order and buy through the book list.
http://infolabwww.kub
.nl:2080/calvin_hobbes
Rachel Prior, 11

Doom Patrol

Straight from the pages of the well known DC Comic *The Doom Patrol*, the series that started in 1987 and unfortunately ended in 1995, this is a great site. It contains summaries of all 87 Doom Patrol issues, and a host of front covers and various examples of Doom Patrol art. Of special interest to Doom Patrol

fans is a preview of the Flex Mentallo mini-series.
http://www.rpi.edu/~bulloj
/Doom_Patrol/DoomPatrol
.html
Philip Reilly, 12

Generation X

The idea of this page is to get non-comic book readers to pick up a Marvel Comic, and hey, you might even like it! On this page you can read the whole of the Generation X #1 comic, which is a very good comic book. The page itself was put up in 1994, and so may be a bit outdated.
http://www.st.nepean.uws
.edu.au/stuff/genx
Philip Reilly, 12

Hergé and Tintin

You may not have heard of Tintin, but in England and the rest of Europe he is a popular cartoon character. Tintin is a boy detective who

Location: http://members.aol.com/Darkhugh/spmcomic.htm

Spidey's Online!!!

DH's Den

MARVEL ONLINE

goes on great adventures with his dog Snowy. This is a simple site, with some pictures of the characters and some info about the author, George Remi (known as Hergé). The text is in French and English, and there are loads of good links to books and other stuff. The Albums Tintin page lists all the Tintin books, and gives a picture from each one. It's a good site.
http://www.du.edu/~tomills /tintin.html
David Reilly, 10

Spiderman

This is one of the best Spiderman sites on the Net. Here, you can read about Marvel comics, reviews of recent stories, and up-to-date information on all kinds of news related to Spiderman. Take a look at Spiderman Resources where you can find links to quizzes, images, sounds, stories, and more.
http://minuteman.com /spiderman
Melissa Edwards, 14

Darkhugh's Den Spider-Man Page

Another Spider-Man page by a Die-Hard fan. Not any ordinary Spider-Man page, this one is quite the oppo-

site—totally out of the ordinary! Keep up-to-date on the newest issues, the Clone Debate, and for that matter, find out what the Clone Debate is. Learn about the greatest Spider-Man artists ever, and who to avoid. See the latest and the greatest information on the Spider-Man movie, and even how to alter your Windows to look like the home of Spider-Man.
http://members.aol.com /Darkhugh/spmcomic.htm
David Lindsay, 11

Superman

It's a bird! It's a plane! It's Web site Superman! If you're a huge fan, come here to learn about each character, including the scoop on their private lives. It lets kids explore the mind of Supes.
http://web.syr.edu/~ajgould /superman.html
Ai Kurobi, 12

Superman Radio Serial

Comic book heaven! Real radio sound is the key here as this site promises you will hear an old radio broadcast of a Superman episode. You have to download some software and I didn't get it to work but I bet it is neat if you do. It is about before TV when all kids had was sound. Get some help from someone who knows how to do this stuff and it will be worth the time to go here.
http://www.dc comics .com/radio
Amy Schroeder, 10

The Arthur Homepage!

This site has everything you ever wanted to know about

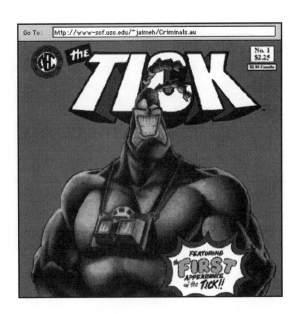

Arthur, Tick's brave sidekick. They make sure to point out that he is a moth and not a bunny! The coolest thing about this page is that there are links to a lot of other Tick pages that have pictures and audio clips that can be downloaded. If you are a Tick fan, this is a good place to start.
http://www.welch.jhu.edu /homepages/harry/html /arthur.html
Kelsey Mays, 11

The Incredibly Complete Tick Links Page!

This strange site could actually be fun if you'd give it a try. It has a long list of links pertaining to the Tick. You'll find links to sounds, videos, sites, and more. Go ahead, try it! You never know where it could lead!

http://www.intranet.org /~maggi/tick.html

Melissa Edwards, 14

Wonder Woman World Wide Web Page

You start off on this page and you'll notice that it is regularly updated. Wonder Woman's Web page has also got some great graphics! However, it is best viewed with Netscape 2.0, so if you have yet to upgrade, you may want to consider that many of the images and text "surprises" are not viewed best with anything less than 2.0. Some of the "extras" this site has are: a collectibles page with descriptions and photos of the memorabilia that is talked about, and upcoming WW conventions. If you are a Wonder Woman fan, or even if you are just a curious Web browser, stop by and have a look.

http://wonderwoman .simplenet.com

Kellie Vaughn, 13

Chapter

4 The Laboratory

i love the Internet because there is always something new, something interesting. It's beyond impossible to get bored when you have the Internet. I find it frustrating that it takes a long time for things to load, but that's not much. I also find it frustrating that some people will put links to things that don't exist (example: I searched for *Star Wars* sheet music, found some, there was a big page with a "click here," but the music still had to be scanned in)... Also, kids hate to be bored, and the Internet is a sure cure for boredom.

Sarah Alderdice 10
CRANFORD, NEW JERSEY, USA

Top Sites

1. **The Palace**
   http://www.thepalace.com

2. **MSN Kids**
   http://www.msn.com/kids

3. **Little Jason's Games Page**
   http://www.fn.net/~jmayans/games.htm

4. **American Girl**
   http://www.pleasantco.com

5. **Calvin and Hobbes Comic Gallery**
   http://infolabwww.kub.nl:2080/calvin_hobbes

Location : http://www.pleasantco.com/

Pleasant Company For Amer

American Girl

The AMERICAN GIRLS CLUB

For American Girls

Catalogue

AG Magazine / The American Girls Club / Pleasant Company Catalogue / Talk to Us

WebCrawler SELECT

© Copyright 1996 Pleasant Company

Experiments

They're all about trying, trying again, try- try- trying again, and then changing the world

It's a Mad, Mad World

Dear Mad Scientist: I would like to know if I was in a big metal container with no cracks, and I turned on a torch and then turned it off again, would the light stay? I asked my mum and my teacher and they could not answer.—Dieter

Hello Dieter: As soon as the source of light is extinguished, it will be totally dark. The reason is that photons are travelling at 186,000 miles/sec and are absorbed by the container. The "torch" to me, means a flashlight. A real torch would produce carbon monoxide... don't do it.
—Mad Micro

Mad Scientist Network
http://medinfo.wustl.edu
/uysp/msn

Bill Nye the Science Guy's NYE LABS ONLINE

Bill Nye really knows how to make science fun. If you like science, you'll love this site, which is based on Bill's Seattle-based PBS TV show, *Bill Nye the Science Guy*. Nye Labs Online has every bell and whistle available on the Internet: great graphics, frames, animations, sound, video, and a real-time chat room of science. There is even a Demo of the Day, an experiment you can perform yourself. As Bill likes to say, "Science Rules!"
http://nyelabs.kcts.org
David Lindsay, 11

Virtual Frog Dissection Kit

Why kill a real frog for dissection when you can dissect an animated one online? Take a look at some of the options, such as the internal organs section, the muscle section, and the tissue layer section. Each section describes what you are looking at in each picture. It is very interesting if you have never dissected one, or if you have and just want to take a better look!
http://george.lbl.gov/ITG.hm.pg.docs/dissect/info.html
Joe Conrad, 13

You Can with Beakman and Jax

A cool place for us to go! You really need to appreciate some of the stranger things in life to cherish this location—for example, a recipe to make fake snot. Previews of future TV shows are available. While there are many strange entries, there are great pictures of outer space. Finally, for some weird and wonderful links, try the bottom of his leg!
http://www.nbn.com/youcan
Rachel Prior, 11

Mad Scientist Network

This page asks the question, "Does wearing a rubber band on your wrist minimize motion sickness?" The answer... You have to visit the page to find out! Have you ever just had to know the answer to a question? Well, that's what the Mad Scientist Network is all about. You can submit questions and have the answer emailed to you. You can also see a list of the Mad Scientist's questions, view the current questions, visit the Mad Scientist Library or Join the Network. Just be careful not to go Mad over this page!
http://medinfo.wustl.edu/~ysp/MSN
Adam Michaels, 13

How to Make Mice

For a long time, people believed that living creatures could come to life from nonliving things. They would look at rotting meat, see maggots in it, and conclude that the maggots grew out of the meat. A seventeenth-century recipe for creating mice required placing sweaty underwear and husks of wheat in an open jar for 21 days. It wasn't until 1859 that Louis Pasteur convinced the world that it was impossible for any creature to be born without parents. Pasteur put meat broth in an S-shaped flask, in which air could get in but heavier-than-air microorganisms could not. No organisms grew, as he expected.

The Slow Death of Spontaneous Generation
http://www.gene.com/ae/AB/BC/Spontaneous_Generation.html

Inventions

A great inventor once said that people are born geniuses but are taught not to be. If that's the case, the younger you are the closer you are to being a genius!

Q: What silly question inspired the instant camera?

A: "Why do we have to wait to see the pictures?" The question was asked by the daughter of Edward Land as he was taking pictures of his family. Good question! Land thought, and he invented the Polaroid camera soon after.

Creativity
http://www.quantumbooks
.com/Creativity.html

Albert Einstein Online

Do you like Albert Einstein? If you do, visit this site. It has general information, Einstein writings, quotes, pictures, miscellaneous links and general announcements. You'll find a link to a page that tells you whether or not the original Theory of Relativity manuscripts have been sold. Or how about a link to the Einstein CyberCard where you can sign his birthday card? The best part about this page are the links to pictures of Einstein.

http://www.sas.upenn.edu/~smfriedm/einstein.html
Adam Michaels, 13

Women Inventors

This is an interesting site for doing a report. It has lots of interesting information about women inventors. There are no pictures and it could have been more interesting if there were, but some of the stories are good. So read it anyway, then when someone asks you to name an inventor, you can give a better answer than Thomas Edison.
http://www.si.sgi.com/organiza/museums/nmah/homepage/lemel/Wmvent.htm
Kelsey Mays, 11

Learn to Be an Inventor

Have you been dreaming about some new type of pop, or how about a flying car? If you don't think you have what you need to be an inventor, think again! Read about such famous inventors as Ben Franklin and Richard G. Drew. Find out how YOU can become an inventor. Some of the coolest things were invented by kids like me and you!
http://mustang.coled.umn.edu/inventing/inventing.html
Joe Conrad, 13

Alexander Graham Bell's Path to the Telephone

This is the best Alexander Graham Bell page ever. The #1 feature of this page is one of the first things to load. All you have to do is point and click to see a map of Bell's progress. You start at 1872 and end up in 1876. You can even read Bell's notebook. Cool!
http://jefferson.village.virginia.edu/albell/homepage.html
Adam Michaels, 13

Mistakes Made Her Rich

When she was 17, Bette Nesmith Graham (who is the mother of one of The Monkees!) got a job as a secretary. The only problem was that she had bad typing skills, and in the pre-computer era, this was a big problem. When electric typewriters began to be sold in the 1950s and the ribbons changed, she found she could no longer erase her mistakes. One day while she was out on the street, she saw some painters painting over the flaws in their work. She decided to do the same thing. By 1956, Graham was making batches of "Mistake Out" in her home. She changed the name to "Liquid Paper", and by 1975, it was sold in 31 countries.

Inventor of the Week Archives
http://web.mit.edu/afs/athena.mit.edu/org/i/invent/www/archive.html

Disasters

Natural disasters don't happen often, but when they do, Mother Nature doesn't mess around. Learn more about her terrifying displays of power on the Web

Automated Atlantic Hurricane & Storm Tracking

Every three hours, check back to this site. This computer system checks and tracks storms, hurricanes, and other disturbances in the Earth's atmosphere in and around the Atlantic area of the United States. View up-to-date information as it becomes available. This is a good way to tell if your class picnic at the park will be cancelled or if you should start boarding up the windows on the house!
http://www.terrapin.com/hurricane
Joe Conrad, 13

Earthquake Bulletin

Doing a school project on the world's most recent earthquakes? You might want to check out this site. Although it's lacking in neat graphics, it does have area and world maps showing the locations of the various earthquakes, and gives information on the exact location of the epicenter, strength, etc. For the younger kid, it may be rather boring without the help of a parent as there is a lot of text to read.
http://www.civeng.carleton.ca/cgi-bin/quakes
Nykki-Lynn Smelser, 10

Volcano World

When you first get to Volcano World, a cute volcano welcomes you. You can choose to go to many different links, some of which include What is Volcano World?, Kids Door, and many, many others. You know where you are because the site informs you what it's about at the beginning. Kids Door is really neat! You can view fan mail, art, games, you name it! So go visit Volcano World! And say "hi" to "Rocky" for me!
http://volcano.und.nodak.edu
Morgan Balavage, 12

Forest Fire Fighting Hotshot Crew

Follow a group of U.S. forest firefighters through a fire. Read along as they talk about walking into a fire to stop it from spreading. Along with the text are a series of pictures depicting what they see. Follow other links to fire-related sites after learning more about Mother Nature's heroes.
http://www.sover.net/~kenandeb/fire/hotshot.html
Joe Conrad, 13

Space Travel

Forty years ago, astronauts were science fiction. Now they make regular trips aboard the space shuttle. What next? Stay online and find out

I Want to Be an Astronaut When I Grow Up

There's really nothing to it. All you have to do is be an American citizen, in good physical condition, with perfect eyesight. The easier way is to become a mission specialist, and for that, you should get a Ph.D. Get your pilot's license. Along the way, don't experiment with nose rings: NASA likes people who are clean-cut. Get accepted to the astronaut's one year training program. Do well there. Even then...

How to Become an Astronaut
http://www.ksc.nasa.gov /facts/faq12.html

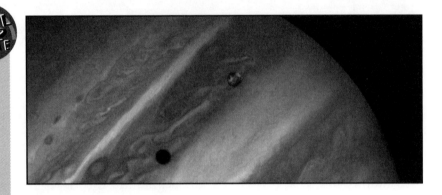

NASA—Homepage

Here you'll find links to the various NASA Web sites and centers. Search NASA's library of top-rated pages, or find answers to some of the most frequently asked space-related questions. There are lots of downloadable audio and image files from space. Check out the most recent Hubble Telescope images, too. Find out about space station experiments and aeronautics research and then link to Today@NASA and find out details of the latest NASA news or follow the next shuttle's preparations, countdown to launch, space mission, and splashdown. It's all here at NASA's homepage.

http://www.nasa.gov/NASA_homepage.html
Nykki-Lynn Smelser, 10

The Ultimate Fieldtrip: An Astronaut's View of the Earth

If you like space, this site is THE site for you! There are descriptions of what it's like to be in space and looking down on earth, pictures of the earth, etc. The site is very well set out, and looks very nice too.
http://ersaf.jsc.nasa.gov/uft/uft1.html
Bronwyn Lee, 12

U. S. Space Camp

Search for: "u._s._space_camp_review.wri" searching... searching... searching... Document Found! Boy that computer sure works slo... Oh, hi! A review on U.S. Space Camp: Here you can find out lots of stuff about Space Camp. You can download Quicktime movies, register for Space Camp, check out cool links, make comments, and more! You can look at cool pictures of things you would find at Space Camp like "Space Shot," "Misson to Mars," and "Journey to Jupiter." Blast-off!!!
http://www.spacecamp.com
David Sawchak, 7

Team Spirit

The Internet has just about everything a kid could want to find. It is so vast you could spend a lifetime surfing it and never get bored! However, it can get frustrating waiting for your computer to link up with a popular page, and because it's so big, you can waste a lot of time searching for something that interests you without knowing exactly where to look. That's why a guidebook for kids is such a great idea. Perhaps the best thing about the Internet is the chance it gives you to make new friends across the world.

Philip Reilly 12
MILTON-KEYNES, ENGLAND

1. **Oasis**
   http://www.oasisinet.com

2. **Kidspace**
   http://main.aisp.net/text/kid.htm

3. **The Simpsons**
   http:// Web .cs.mun.ca
   /~jbishop/simpsons.html

4. **X-Files**
   http://www.thex-files.com/index.htm

5. **TCC 24 Seven**
   http://www.tcc.co.uk/inside/index.html

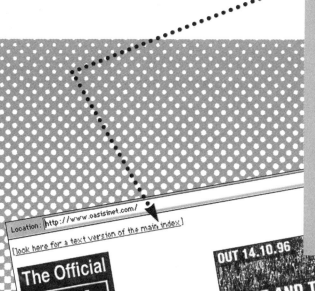

Location: http://www.oasisinet.com/

[look here for a text version of the main index]

The Official **oasis** Home Page

sponsored by:

controlroom

OUT 14.10.96

THERE AND THEN

Cycling

Whether you're flying along a stretch of pavement or jumping stumps down a mountainside—the newest accessory that's sure to help your performance is the biking Web site

Mark Twain's Big Adventure

In the 1880s, Mark Twain learned how to ride a high-wheeled bicycle. He said the ride was very bumpy. Roads weren't smooth back then, and tires were solid, like tricycle tires. It was also risky—the first bikes had no brakes. In his essay "Taming the Bicycle," Twain wrote "Get a bicycle, you will not regret it, if you live."

Taming the Bicycle
http://www.teachersoft.com /Library/lit/twain /whatsman/essay14.htm

Cyber Cyclery

Cyber Cyclery is one of the best Internet resources for serious bikers! From the high-tech main page, you can click on links to find out the latest bicycle news. If you want some paper information on bicycles, you can order the enCYCLEopedia. There is even a bulletin board for bike enthusiasts to post about bicycles for sale, biking problems, and the best way to warm up before biking! The Web site is filled with graphics, so prepare for a long wait.
http://cyclery.com
Carol Scott, 13

The Big Ring

This site is great if you're into cycling, BUT ONLY if you're into cycling! The Big Ring contains all the latest cycling news. If this site doesn't quench your thirst for cycling information then it provides tons of other bike links to satisfy you. There's lots of nutritional info for all you bike racers out there, as well as a diet plan and a guide to what to wear.
http://nsns.com/BigRing
Philip Reilly, 12

Pedaling History—The Burgwardt Bicycle Museum

"There's more to bicycles than you may think," announces the opening text as you enter this online museum. That is just what you will discover as you browse around. When you start this "tour in history" you will be greeted with the opening image of the bicycle's evolution from pre-dino days to the present. There are great, brief descriptions of how each level in the bicycle's history came about, and how it changed human travels. If you are a bike lover, or are just interested in learning more about the history of the bike... look here.
http://members.aol.com/bicyclemus/bike_museum PedHist.htm
Kellie Vaughn, 13

Q: Who eats more, a professional bicyclist or a professional football player?

A: The bicyclist. The average professional bicyclist eats 8,730 calories a day, more than twice the amount eaten by the average pro football player (4,047).

Do It Sports Past Trivia: Mountain Biking
http://gnn522.gnnhost.com /chat/past-mtb.html

GET THIS!

The popularity of bicycles with women in the 1890s not only gave women more mobility, it changed their wardrobe. Susan B. Anthony said that "the bicycle has done more for the emancipation of women than anything else in the world."

Pedaling History—
The Burgwardt Bicycle Museum
http://members.aol.com /bicyclemus/bike_museum /PedHist.htm

Baseball

If you can't understand the appeal of watching a bunch of men toss a ball around a dusty field, it's time you took yourself out to the online ballpark

Trivia

Q: Who won the 1981 NL Cy Young Award?

A: Fernando Valenzuela.

Q: What is the diameter of the on-deck circle, according to the official rules?

A: Five feet.

Q: Who won the World Series in 1946?

A: St. Louis Cardinals.

The Bullpen Ace Trivia Game
http://www.dtd.com/ace

ESPNET SportsZone: Major League Baseball

Even though it's set up a lot like the sports section of a newspaper, ESPNET SportsZone surpasses the quality and depth of a newspaper when it comes to Major League Baseball. "What's the headline?" may be a typical question to a newspaper subscriber, but to an Internet jockey, it's "What's the headline, and yesterday's headline? Heck, what's June 1, 1992's headline?" Everything you could possibly want in a baseball Web page can be found here.
http://espnet.sportszone.com/mlb
David Lindsay, 11

National Baseball Hall of Fame

Any baseball fan knows what the Baseball Hall of Fame is. Those who do and those who want to find out, can visit this site and learn more. When was it built? How big is it? All your questions are answered.
http://www.enews.com/bas_hall_fame
David Lindsay, 11

Little League Baseball

Are you a Little League player? Or a parent of a Little League player? Find out tricks on how to help that swing, or in a parent's case, how to coach a team of Little League players. There are links, tips for youngsters and adults, an FAQ page, a Little League War Stories section (which is a section full of interesting Little League stories) and even a 1-800 number so you can have all your questions answered.

http://www2.netdoor.com/~jtravis

David Lindsay, 11

Bullpen Ace Trivia Game

The Bullpen Ace Trivia Game is one of the best trivia games on the Net. Despite the very long loading time, it is still a great site. For true fans, this site has fairly hard questions.

http://www.dtd.com/ace

Jeff Little, 13

Netsite: http://www.infi.net/~moxie/nlb/nlb.html

75 Years Of Glory

NEGRO LEAGUES BASEBALL ONLINE ARCHIVES

©1996 NLBOA

MAGELLAN 3 STAR SITE

c|net BEST of the Web

TEAMS OF THE NEGRO LEAGUES

A League of Their Own

Did you know that some of the greatest baseball players of all time weren't allowed to play in the Major Leagues just because they were black? Until 1945, when a rookie named Jackie Robinson was signed by the Brooklyn Dodgers, African Americans played in separate baseball leagues. One of the greatest baseball players of this century, a pitcher named Satchel Paige, threw so hard that he would sometimes knock off his catcher's glove—or even knock him down! While standing at the pitcher's mound, Paige could hit a line of soda pop bottles at the baseline and not miss any.

The Negro Leagues of Baseball
http://www.ecnet.net/users /murjd5/baseball

Basketball

Rodman, Jordan, Shaq, Hardaway—professional basketball has become as big as the guys who play it, too. Jump on the b-ball bandwagon on the Net

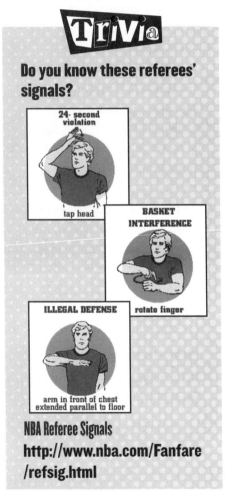
Official Dennis Rodman Fan Club

This Web page on Dennis Rodman is like him—crazy. You can go and read about Dennis's hair and you can even see pictures of Rodman's hair archive!
You can join the Dennis Rodman Fan Club. You can find out about his life off the court as well as on. The famous Chicago Bull's player has a fantastic Web site page which can entertain you for hours!

http://www.texas.net/users/pmagal
Elizabeth Wolff, 12

What Hair Do You Like Best?

This is not a site to bookmark, but everyone should visit at least once and vote on which of Dennis Rodman's hair colors they like the best. There are pictures of ten different choices and the percentage of voters who have picked each color.

There are a few links to other pages here also. One is to a great Michael Jordan page and one is to a Sports Poll page where you get to tell who you think is better, the Lakers or the Bulls.

http://www.worldstar.com/~britnath/color.htm

Kelsey Mays, 11

Jordan & Chicago Bulls Homepage

There is a lot of information here, including a lot of stuff I didn't know about them, even though I am a regular Bulls fan. But if you were looking for something other than information and background I would not recommend it. More famous clips from the Bulls games should be shown.

http://www.apc.net/km

Tweba Sargeant, 12

The NBA

This is the only site where you can receive the real, up-to-date information and standings on your favorite teams. In the League offices, meet the men and women who set up this whole basketball scene and see the behind the scenes action as they go to work. Find out in advance who will be featured on this week's NBA Inside Stuff at the On The Air section.

http://www.nba.com

Joe Conrad, 13

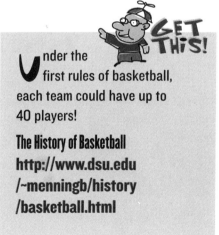

Under the first rules of basketball, each team could have up to 40 players!

The History of Basketball
http://www.dsu.edu
/~menningb/history
/basketball.html

If you are a Michael Jordan fan, then this is a site to visit! It has his statistics and links to other great Jordan pages. The best thing is that at this site there are links to all of the stuff they could find to download about Michael. You can download pictures, movies, or sounds from the Downloading Page.

http://www.cs.technion.ac.il /~yvonne/jordan.html

Kelsey Mays, 11

Location: http://members.

michael jordan!

Location: http://www.apo.net/km/newlogo.jpg

Michael Jordan and Chicago Bulls Homepage

Jordan Page

NOTHING BUT NET!

Football

It may be played on AstroTurf rather than grass these days, and indoors as often as out, but the thrill of the long bomb, the Blitz, and the Hail Mary remains the same

Q: Who was the coach of the losing team in Superbowl XXVIII?

A: Marv Levy. Levy's Bill's lost their second straight Super Bowl to the Cowboys, 30-13.

Q: What year was the first NFL game broadcast on radio?

A: A Bears-Lions game in 1934.

Q: Who won the Rose Bowl after the 1989 Season?

A: The USC Trojans.

2 Minute Warning
http://www.dtd.com/tmw

Junior Seau Kidzone

Are you a fan of Tiaina Seau, the famous NFL Football player? Well, here's where you can test your knowledge, and learn about Junior Seau's history, language, and country.
http://www.juniorseau.org/kidzone/kidzone.html
David Lindsay, 11

ESPNET SportsZone College Football

Another well-designed Web site filled with lots of college football news stories and many other features. You can take a look at "Spring Drills '96" for a comprehensive look at every

Division I-A college team. If you want to reminisce about the '95–'96 season, you can "revisit the bowls," or if you're not very experienced in the game you can look "inside the rule book." Well worth a visit.

http://espnet.sportszone.com/nfl
Philip Reilly, 12

TSN: College Football

Want to know the latest info on college football? Check out the NCAA Senior Bowl All-Star Classic, the latest news on who's being traded, and more. This page is mainly results of games, and future plans of games, so unless you watch a lot of football, this page will indeed bore you.

http://www.sportsnetwork.com:80/filter/filter.cgi
/collegefootball/index.html
David Lindsay, 11

Steve Young

Another great site dedicated to a football player—this time, Steve Young, quarterback for the San Francisco 49ers. With all Steve Young's essential information and even all his statistics, this page is definitely for fans and card collectors. There are pictures, lots of them, so it will help you a lot if you're making your own NFL page.

http://www.ece.orst.edu/~bevans/sy.html
David Lindsay, 11

Lions and Tigers and Sooners?

COOL KID SITE

Jets and Lions make sense as football team names, but why are the Oklahoma Sooners called the Sooners? In 1889, the Oklahoma Territory opened up for settlement. Everyone rushed in to claim the new land. One of the rules of the government giveaway was that everyone must start at the same time, which would be marked by the sound of a cannon. Afterward, those who rode out when the cannon went off were called Boomers, while those who started before the cannon were called Sooners. Teams at the University of Oklahoma began to be called by that name in 1908, after a pep club named the Sooner Rooters.

The University of Oklahoma Athletic Department
http://www.ou.edu/athweb

Horseback Riding

There's a lot more to horseback riding than just hopping on and saying "giddyup." There's biology, physics, even history, involved. Saddle up your browsers and see for yourself

They Don't Horse Around

You may think that a jockey's life is not that hard. You just hop on your horse, go around the track a few times, and you're done for the week. Not so. The typical jockey usually works long hours, and may even live at the stables and do the same chores as the stablehands. There are a lot of meetings too, in which he or she analyzes videotapes of previous races, or discusses the horse's performance.

Jockey
http://www.edna.edu.au
/cgi-bin/nph-jobguide
/T.R.A.AH.J391513

The Hay Net: An Exhaustive List of Horse Sites on the Internet

Nearly all children in the world believe they love horses and need one of their own. Included in this site is a guide for dressage, general resources, veterinary courses, and stable management. Maybe you will change your mind about owning a horse after you read about all the work involved. There are also personal home pages that other horse lovers have done.
http://www.freerein.com/haynet
Rachel Prior, 11

Horse Country

Horse Country is absolutely the best Web page about horses on the Internet. From the clear photographs to the many horse links, this site is definitely worth visiting! If you're a beginning rider, you can learn the techniques of riding, the clothes to wear, and join a horse club like HOCK (Horse Owners Club for Kids). The more serious riders can join an email mailing list dedicated to horses and riding them—the Junior Riders list. And everyone can look for pen pals with the Horse Penpal Page! Once you have explored the site, be sure to come back later—it's always being updated.
http://www.pathology.washington.edu/Horse/index.html
Carol Scott, 13

A Rodeo Cowboy's Homepage

This page is interesting to say the least! It gives a fairly detailed insight into the life of Brick, a rodeo cowboy. Brick likes to ride bulls! He tried it once and now he's hooked. Brick's page includes the answers to the top three questions a cowboy hears: "Yes. I am a real cowboy," "No, I don't mean mechanical bulls," "No, that works just fine. Everything else hurts, but that still works." It also includes a journal of all his rodeos so far, and other "cool" links to cowboy pages. The most boring part has to be the "original writings" section, which is not about rodeos and not very interesting. But you are invited to add to it, so maybe you could liven it up!
http://www.umd.umich.edu/~reasons
Philip Reilly, 12

The Lost Horses of Tibet

No matter how many horses you have ridden, it's almost certain you've never ridden a Riwoche. The tiny horses stand under four feet high, and while they are used by Tibetan locals in the remote Riwoche Valley of Tibet, they were unknown to anyone else until last year. A French expedition, on the trail of another rare species, just happened to run across them.

CNN—Tiny Ancient Horses Found in Tibet
http://www-cgi.cnn.com /WORLD/9511/tibet_pony

Pro Wrestling

It may not be real, but who cares? Neither are the movies. What's important is the excitement of watching these outrageous bruisers chase each other around the ring

Pro Wrestling, Zorro Style

In Mexico, pro-wrestlers wear masks. The masks were inspired by Aztec traditions of masked warriors. A mask is considered the wrestler's prized possession. To be unmasked in a match is the ultimate humiliation, but very few will make it through an entire career with their mask and anonymity preserved.

Pro Wrestling FAQ
http://emunix.emich.edu
/~macika/Wrestling/faq.htm

WWWF Grudge Match

This is one of the wackiest pages you will ever visit. It opens up with a strange and silly argument. For instance, who can drink more, Ted Kennedy or Boris Yeltsin? Next, is an argument between two men (Steve and Brian) who are much like two announcers on TSN: always arguing. After the two point out several reasons why their decision is better, you get to choose. After you decide, you are taken to a page where there are all the votes are tallied up. Wanna see Chewbacca vs. Worf? *Die Hard*'s John McClane versus the Death Star!
http://cheme.cornell.edu:80/~slevine
David Lindsay, 11

The Wrestling Network

The Wrestling Network divides its site into a few different sections. The leagues include WWF, WCW, EXW, and Japan pro wrestling. They also have newsletters for all of them. The Wrestling Network also has excellent graphics! An up-and-coming site for sure!
http://members.aol.com/wrestnet/wnindex/wnindex.html
Jeff Little, 13

Otto "Hack-Man" Heuer Pro Wrestling Page

Get the "Hack-Man's" ideas about why wrestling went down the drain. Also, find out if this whole wrestling thing is fake, predetermined, and if any fans care. At the bottom of his page are links to a WWF site, and a few other leagues. After each link is a short review of the organization and why it is good or just plain ridiculous. Go check it out!

http://www.tc.umn.edu/nlhome/g249/heuer004

Joe Conrad, 13

Q: How did Hulk Hogan get started in wrestling?

A: Perhaps the best-known wrestler of our time, Hulk Hogan was just a part-time bouncer and full-time bank teller named Terry Bollea until he was discovered by wrestler Jack Brisco.

Q: How big is Hulk Hogan?

A: Six foot five, 300 pounds.

Q: What are the Hulk Hogan commandments?

A: 1. Train hard.
   2. Eat your vitamins.
   3. Say your prayers.

Who Is Hulk Hogan and Why Doesn't Anyone Like Him?
http://www.deakin.edu.au /~bramsey/wrestle3.html

PRO WRESTLING
The Maniac's

Location: http://www.pro-wrestling.com/main.jpg

Location: http://Adscape.com/wrestling/

FREE WEB TOOLS!
CLICK   HERE   NOW

Professional
Wrestling

ONLINE   MUSEUM

This site is best viewed with Netscape Navigator 3.0 or Microsoft Explorer 3.0

Welcome to the Professional Wrestling Online Museum
(formerly known as the R.S.P-W Web Page.)

Location: http://www.kudonet.com/~ximed/flex.JPG

WWF Site

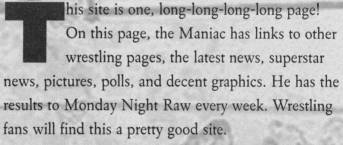

This site is one, long-long-long-long page! On this page, the Maniac has links to other wrestling pages, the latest news, superstar news, pictures, polls, and decent graphics. He has the results to Monday Night Raw every week. Wrestling fans will find this a pretty good site.

http://pages.prodigy.com/Q/K/B/QKNM53B/maniac.htm

Jeff Little, 13

Soccer

It's been the world's favorite sport for years. Now, the U.S. is finally catching on to the fun—probably because a lot of American kids are now playing the game

GET THIS!

Rough soccer games are nothing new. In fact, soccer used to be so tough, kings of England banned the sport repeatedly—beginning in the 1100s!

Planet Soccer—Origins of the Game
http://web-usa.com/soccer/Shistori.htm

Villa Soccer Club

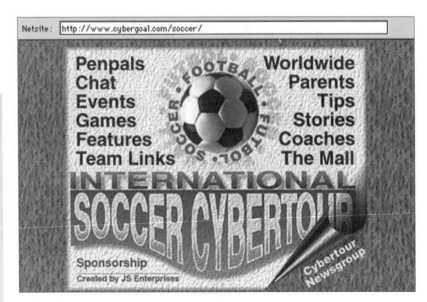

Netsite: http://www.cybergoal.com/soccer/

Penpals
Chat
Events
Games
Features
Team Links

Worldwide
Parents
Tips
Stories
Coaches
The Mall

FOOTBALL · SOCCER · FUTBOL

INTERNATIONAL SOCCER CYBERTOUR

Cybertour Newsgroup

Sponsorship
Created by JS Enterprises

International Soccer Cybertour

This is one of the best soccer sites on the Web. The title logo doubles as an interactive image map which allows you to go to a number of links. There is also a rather cool animation you might want to check out. If you like soccer you'll enjoy lots of this site's features. One of the great things about the Net is the opportunity to make friends worldwide. This soccer site's

pen pal section puts you in touch with other soccer nuts around the globe. You can read the stories people have put up, and look at photos of teams from all over the world. This site allows you to have your say, especially in the chat forum.
http://www.cybergoal.com/soccer

The Soccer Patch

The Soccer Patch is a place where kids can view soccer patches which represent teams, towns, and tournaments. But who exactly wants to see a load of soccer patches? It is a well-designed site, just not very interesting. If you would like the world to see your team's patch, you can send it in, and it could be chosen as "Patch of the Month."
http://soccerpatch.com/SOCCER/soccer.html

RETE Soccer News

This page is part of RETE's international soccer site. It may help to know Italian, since half of it is written in that language, but most of the Italian has been translated into English. The site has all the latest news, views, and goals from around the world, both international and club matches. There are lots of links to other soccer sites for all you soccer fanatics out there. But surely the best things offered by this site are the QuickTime or AVI movies of all the latest goals from international games. For soccer fans this is a brilliant site!
http://www.vol.it/RETE_/01/00045.html
All soccer sites reviewed by Philip Reilly, 12

The World's Game

Unlike many sports, varieties of soccer have been invented by many people in different parts of the world.

— In North America in the 1600s, Indians played a ball game called pasuckuakohowog, which meant, "they gather to play ball with the foot." Goals were one mile apart, with 1,000 players on the field at one time!

—In China, a soccer-like game was played during an emperor's birthday celebration—in 2500 B.C.!

—Early Pacific Islanders played ball games using coconuts, oranges, and pig bladders!

Planet Soccer—Origins of the Game
http://web-usa.com/soccer/Shistori.htm

Make a Splash!

Whether you like to dive in it, paddle through it, sail across it, or swim in it, water is a great place to have fun. Get your feet wet, dive right in and surf these sites

The world record for the 50 meter freestyle swim is 21.81 seconds, set by Tom Jager of the United States in 1990. Fifty meters is about 150 feet. How fast is 21.81 seconds? About the same amount of time it probably took you to read this paragraph!

ESPN Sportzone:
Swimming World Records
http://espnet.sportszone
.com/editors/atlanta96
/sports/wim/wr2.html

The Dog's Scuba Page

Have you ever scuba dived? Sounds like fun! At this site you can learn about scuba diving or go to another scuba page from a list of links! If you are an expert, you can subscribe to your favorite diving magazines or join some clubs at other diving pages. Great fun for all.
http://www.scubadog.com
Rachel Prior, 11

SailWeb

Sailing, sailing! Feel that fresh sea breeze on your face. This site is absolutely the best. You can even buy a boat or join a yacht club! Are you planning to go sailing, but think there may be a big storm? Well, no need to worry, you can check the weather right here at their weather page. You can also visit pages completed by other sailing lovers!
http://www.bga.com/~dkern/sail.html
Rachel Prior, 11

Windsurfer.com

Really neat little pictures on the first screen caught my attention and made me check out the links. I like to swim and I see windsurfers at a lake I go to, so I checked out the beginners link and read about how to windsurf. This is the spot for you to go if you like or want to know more about windsurfing.
http://www.windsurfer.com
Amy Schroeder, 10

Surfrider Foundation USA

Surfrider is packed full of surfer information. Read the Surf report for marine and weather forecasts including storm-tracking and satellite images in and around the world's coasts. Find out wave heights and buoy readings from coastal areas.
http://www.sdsc.edu/SDSC/Partners/Surfrider/main.htm
Nykki-Lynn Smelser, 10

@queous: Sports and Recreation Swimming and Diving

A wonderful site dedicated to the fine art of swimming and diving. The Web page is by far the best site, in terms of resources and information, on water recreation.
http://www.aqueous.com/aq78.html
Kellie Vaughn, 13

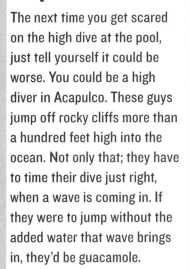

High Divers of Acapulco

The next time you get scared on the high dive at the pool, just tell yourself it could be worse. You could be a high diver in Acapulco. These guys jump off rocky cliffs more than a hundred feet high into the ocean. Not only that; they have to time their dive just right, when a wave is coming in. If they were to jump without the added water that wave brings in, they'd be guacamole.

Hot Wired! World Beat—Rough Guide—Acapulco
http://www.hotwired.com /rough/mexico/acapulco /acapulco/city.html#divers

Extreme Wheels

Once upon a time roller skates were clunky lumps of metal you strapped onto your shoes. These days they are hi-tech, design classics. And they're much, much more fun

Cones + Wheels: The Inline Skating Slalom Page

Are you an inline skating fan? Then this page is for you. Want to know how to slalom like the pros? Now you can find out how to buy your equipment (proper equipment at that), select a spot, set up your own slalom course, and perform on it. Learn the tricks! Even find out how to get into a competition!
http://www.skatecity.com/C+W
David Lindsay, 11

FranTic's Aggro Time

Fran Tic's Aggro Time is Malaysia's premier aggressive skating site. The page's creator, Leon Wong, says the objective of the page is "To show the world the skating scene in Maylasia." If you don't skate, but are interested in getting started up, you can learn all the tricks in Leon and Darren Wong's tutorial page. You can also take a look at Fran Tic's picture gallery, air your views in the forum, or catch up on the info on the pros in the pro closet.
http://www.attitude.org/leon/xtreme
Philip Reilly, 12

Skating the Infobahn

This inline skating super site is full of links! In fact, it is nothing but links. I think it says there are over 700 here, but I only roller skate so I left after about five minutes. It is a fast page and I think a skater could spend all day here.
http://www.skatecity.com/Index
Amy Schroeder, 10

The Orbit

The Orbit is a newsletter for inline skaters which is published about four times a year. This Web site has links to selected articles from the latest issue, as well as from past issues. It also tells you how you can subscribe. A good site for people interested in inline skating, and an interesting example for writers or designers of newsletters on the Web.
http://www.zoom.com/personal/getroll/orbit.html
David Reilly, 10

Q: When were in-line skates invented?

A: They were first invented in the early 1700s and used by Dutch ice skaters. They were reinvented in the early 1980s by ice hockey players looking for a dry-land substitute.

Q: Isn't it dangerous?

A: According to the Consumer Product Safety Commision, people are much more likely to hurt themselves on the softball field or the stairs.

Q: How many skaters are there?

A: An estimated 10 million people now use in-line skates.

Profiling the Inline Skater
http://www.sportsite.com/cedro/sgma/iisa/html/pro&pro.html

Blade Runners

When inline skates first appeared, everyone said it was just a fad. Everyone not on skates, that is. Aggressive skating, or aggro, is the newest development in the world of in-line skating. It was invented by people who thought flying along at 20 miles an hour was too tame. Aggros skate the sides of curbs and walls, and perform other gravity-defying tricks. Look around and find out how to do a fakie, a fakie brainless, and a mctwist (aggro tricks)—and all without so much as a sqweek (accident) or a face-plant (crash).

The Aggressive Skaters Association
http://www.aggroskate.com/asa/menu.html

In-Line Skater Magazine

Whether you're just learning or a bit of a pro at the sport, everything the in-line skater wants/needs to know can be found here. Find out about the various kinds of equipment needed, and how to look after it so it lasts. There are tips and tricks for safe skating as well as other articles of interest. Learn some of the hockey and street-skating lingo, too.
http://www.xcscx.com/skater
Nykki-Lynn Smelser, 10

Hardcore Inline Skating

Inline skating, and everything about it—that's exactly what this page is. Hardcore Inline Skating was the first inline skating page. Before you start, be sure to visit Injuries and Health so you know what to do in all situations: Burns and road/ramp rash, concussions, broken bones, and something for all outdoors folk to watch out for, rabies. Can't quite get that

handrail slide right? Well, a look at Aggressive Skating Help Area couldn't hurt. Hardcore Inline Skating is definitely a cool skating site.

http://www.seas.smu.edu/~justin/inline.html
David Lindsay, 11

Extreme Sports

For extreme sports fans, this is the site for you! This page offers a lot of extreme links, a couple of pictures, and a place to register for Extreme Sports conference boards! It has a pretty cool background, but yellow doesn't mix with extreme sports such as snowboarding, biking, skateboarding, etc. Everything else is extremely interesting.

http://www.taponline.com/tap/sports/extreme/index
Alex Landback, 10

Street Luge—A Skateboard on Steroids

Zoom!!!!! There goes a street luge board flying down the hill next to your house at speeds over 75 miles per hour! Read about the sport that has teens and adults flying down hills, making sharp turns, and using no brakes at all! Although it seems dangerous, read about how many people enjoy the heart-pounding action of street luging. Learn how the riders control these boards, and how they started the sport. This is definitely a page for those thrill-seekers out there.

http://www.extreme-sports.com/luge.htm
Joe Conrad, 13

Chapter

6 Getting Around

i like the fact that I can go all over the world without leaving my house, and I can get lots of information about things for school projects. I think that other kids will like the Internet for the same reasons. It makes our world seem like a very small place. My survey has been interesting, because it's nice to hear from kids in far away places—we're all pretty much the same, and we all like the same things too!

Andrea Bonilla 13

STONEY CREEK, ONTARIO, CANADA

Location: http://www.demon.co.uk/eureka/

EUREKA!

The Museum for Children

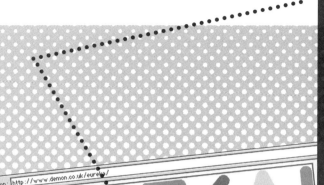

Welcome to Eureka! The Museum for Children.

We are Britain's first hands-on museum, a unique, informal, experiential learning centre housed on two floors in a purpose-built building. The museum has been especially designed for children up to the age of 12, but is suitable for all visitors, and with over 350 interactive exhibits, you'll be amazed at the things you can do.

Where is EUREKA!

Have you ever wondered...

- ...What happens when you eat?
- ...How are TV programs made?
- ...What makes a toilet flush?
- ...How can we reduce the amount of rubbish we throw away?

The answers to all these, and many more, questions will be revealed as you journey through exhibition areas.

On the Road

You're probably counting the days until you get that license and disappear in a cloud of dust. In the meantime, zoom down the information superhighway and search for that perfect car

Ford Door Sedan

When Henry Ford built his first automobile, he forgot one detail: how to get it out of the shed. He decided he would have to knock down a brick wall. Even though it was 2 a.m., he knocked down the wall with an ax and took his "quadricycle" out for its first spin on the streets of Detroit.

A Brief History of 100 Years of the Automobile Industry in the United States
http://www.theauto channel.com/mania /industry/history /chap4.html

Autorama

Rob Coleman is one of the many classic car lovers around the world, only he has a home page displaying cars he loves! Every month, he updates his site. So if you are like Rob, look at a selection of his collection, read about how and why he likes classic cars, and drop him a line through email telling him about how much you like old cars, too!
http://www.designstein.com/autorama
Joe Conrad, 13

Motorville

This is the cybercity of Motorville. It is the online town with everything for auto, truck, and motorcycle lovers. This is the place to take your dad if he is helping you fix up a car. There are shops that offer parts for trucks, cars, and motorcycles of all years. Sign up for a driver's license by entering your name, email address, and your car's name and year, and you can receive email messages when people have parts for sale that will work on your car.

http://www.motorville.com

Joe Conrad, 13

Porsche

A classy site, although the emphasis is on selling you the cars. It includes a short biography of Ferdinand Porsche, the genius behind the great automobiles. The site has all sorts of info about the car company, as well as some pictures of the cars.

http://www.porsche-usa.com

Philip Reilly, 12

Lamborghini

This site is pretty stylish and well-designed (like the cars!). It has loads of posters and pictures of the sleek Lamborghini automobiles, as well as a letter from the president of Automobili Lamborghini, who goes on and on about why you should buy a Lamborghini Diablo and how much better his cars are than all the rest.

http://www.lamborghini.com

Philip Reilly, 12

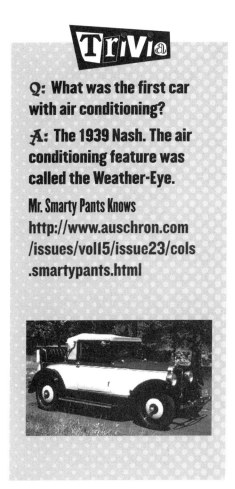

In the Air

The Blackbird doesn't have to live in a tree and Blue Angels aren't always at God's right hand. Pull back your joy stick and hit the skies

USAF Museum Discovery Zone

The Discovery Hangar is where you can have fun learning about the Air Force, airplanes, and how airplanes work. Learn the ABCs of aviation, or the four forces of flight. Discover how a jet engine works, and how aircraft are grouped in categories. Lots of fun for those who enjoy airplanes.
http://www.am.wpafb.af.mil/museum/zone/dz.html
Joe Conrad, 13

The Aerodrome

The Aerodrome is the online version of the Aviation Hall of Fame. Under the section of Hall of Fame Nominations, you can nominate yourself or someone else to be entered into the virtual Hall of Fame by entering their name and aviation achievement. Then test how much you know about aircraft! Take the trivia section quiz and see if you know the name of the aircraft they give you a picture of, then view a really cool picture of an aircraft under the picture of the month.
http://www.airfax.com/aerodrome
Joe Conrad, 13

AMELIA EARHART
1897 - 1937

Amelia Earhart

This site goes into great detail as it brings to you the life of Amelia Earhart. Read about her childhood, her days as a celebrity, and her famous last flight. There's even a collection of theories on what exactly happened to the pilot who disappears during her attempt to fly around the world. See pictures from her childhood and her days of flight.
http://www.ionet.net/~jellenc/ae_intro.html
Melissa Edwards, 14

The Wild Blue Yonder

The eye-catchers of this page are the two stunning graphics on the top. The rest of the page are links to information such as serial numbers from U2s, F-117s, D-21s, and Blackbirds. This page has a list of aviation museums, a show schedule for the Blue Angels and the Thunderbirds, and a page on the decay of the atomic-powered aircraft program. If you choose to go to Elmer's home page, you'll find links to rail- and sea-related sites, too.
http://www.wpi.edu/~elmer/air
Adam Michaels, 13

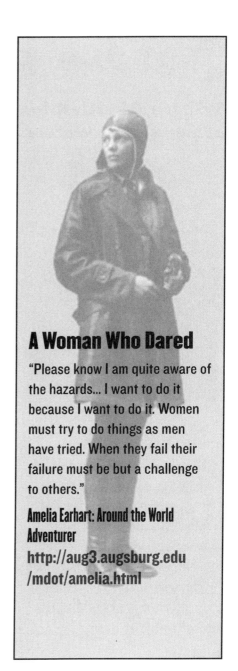

A Woman Who Dared

"Please know I am quite aware of the hazards... I want to do it because I want to do it. Women must try to do things as men have tried. When they fail their failure must be but a challenge to others."

Amelia Earhart: Around the World Adventurer
http://aug3.augsburg.edu/mdot/amelia.html

Across the Sea

Tallships, battleships, subs, tugs, and frigates... they're all afloat on the waters of the World Wide Web

GAMES

Sinking Feeling

Miss. Miss. Hit! There's nothing quite like the search and sink feeling of this classic game, in which you attempt to destroy your opponent's ships before he destroys yours—especially when your opponent is your computer.
http://info.gte.com/gtel/fun /battle/battle.html

Marine Sounds

Download some way cool wave sounds at this marine-oriented site! Sounds of whales, the tide coming in, waves flowing, and a ton more are featured. Then, scroll up or down your screen to view more interesting facts about the sea!
http://www.marineart.com/www/sound.shtml
Joe Conrad, 13

The Tugboat Page

The Tugboat Page is for all of those people that live aboard, work on, or like to watch tugboats. Follow along on a tour of a tugboat being restored or go to the tugboat marketplace, where you can view what some owners need for their tugboat or what they have for sale that you may need. There is also a really neat link to the Internet Yacht Club.
http://worf.ubalt.edu/~bpumphre/tug.html
Joe Conrad, 13

Age of Sail Page

With tons of wonderful links on and about ships, this tops the Web sites for ships of any kind. For starters, the Web page opens with great pictures of ships. With links on other ship pages, great ship photos, and fun facts, this page should be tops on your next Web browse!

http://www.cs.yale.edu/homes/sjl/sail.html
Kellie Vaughn, 13

The Original Titanic Home Page

What can you say that's bad about this page? For anyone who has the slightest curiosity about that huge ship that once sailed the Atlantic waters, take a peek at this terrific site. This page is by far the best Titanic Web page out there, packed full of helpful and educational resources. You won't want to leave!

http://gil.ipswichcity.qld.gov.au/~dalgarry
Kellie Vaughn, 13

Vasa Museum

The Vasa Museum is a museum in Stockholm, built around a seventeenth-century ship that was salvaged in 1961. This is a real fast site—no waiting, if you know what I mean. This page made me want to visit the Vasa Museum because of the really cool ship there. Be sure to click on The Ship link to see a cool photo of it. This site is definitely worth a visit!

http://www.vasamuseet.se/indexeng.html
Amy Schroeder, 10

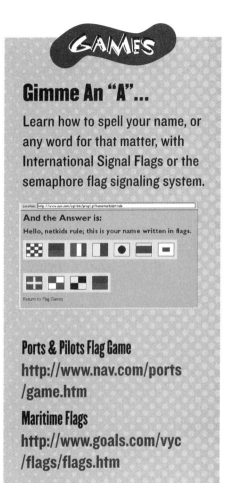

GAMES

Gimme An "A"...

Learn how to spell your name, or any word for that matter, with International Signal Flags or the semaphore flag signaling system.

Ports & Pilots Flag Game
http://www.nav.com/ports/game.htm

Maritime Flags
http://www.goals.com/vyc/flags/flags.htm

On the Tracks

Are trains a thing of the past? Not so long ago, many people thought so. But now, thanks to high-speed rail lines and advanced technology, people are taking a second look at this great form of transportation

Webville & Hypertext Railroad Company

This page is neither a real railroad, nor a railroad company. It is a page with information on old railways and trains. Test your train knowledge in the new trivia section, and discuss railroads a little more in the main office, which contains a huge list of newsgroups to go to. There are also some interesting things about telegraphs and those neat red lights that tell you when a train is coming.
http://www.he.tdl.com/~colemanc/webville.html
Joe Conrad, 13

Penny Bridge: A Rail Station

This site is plain and simple. Go there and hear the melody of a train coming down on the tracks. Choo! Choo!
http://bjr.acf.nyu.edu/railinfo.html
Kelly Roman, 11

Steam Locomotives

Chugga, Chugga... The Steam Locomotives page is all about historical trains! The best things about the page are the detailed, colorful pictures, and the sound clips you can download. Ever wanted to hear what a real train sounds like? You can also read about the trains—their history, and where they are now. There's not much else you can do on this page, but it's a good stop for all train lovers!

http://www.inmind.com/people/teague/steamtrains.html

Carol Scott, 13

Going Underground

In Paris, it's the Metro. Bostonians simply call it the "T." In Chicago, they have the "el," since the Windy City has a mostly elevated train system. In London you take the tube. Subways exist in major cities all over the world, and each system is it's own world. Go explore mass transit in every metropolis around the globe—you won't even need a token.

Subway Navigator
http://metro.jussieu.fr:10001/bin/cities/english

New York City Subway Resources
http://www.k2nesoft.com/subway

T Subway Guide
http://www.bu.edu/images/subway2.rgb.Z

Transit Systems Worldwide
http://www.k2nesoft.com/subway/transitmaps

Museums

Thousands of real-world museums have gone online, including some of the greatest in the world. Whatever interests you, you're likely to find an online museum about it

La Tour Eiffel

The Eiffel Tower was built for the International Exposition of 1889, against the strident opposition of national figures who believed it to be unsafe or ugly, or both. When the exposition concession expired in 1909, demolition of the 989-foot tower was prevented by demonstrating its value as an antenna for the newly developed radio. Additions made for television transmission have added 56 feet to the height. From the topmost of the three platforms, the view extends for 50 miles.

The WebMuseum of Paris
http://sunsite.unc.edu /louvre

The WebMuseum of Paris

You can really visit Paris without even leaving the computer or paying expensive airfares. This is a great site to see pics of Paris along with famous artwork. You can walk around Paris or go on a guided tour, save pics of the Eiffel Tower and visit many museums and educational stuff. The best part is visiting Paris, definitely great for the lovers. Stop harassing your parents for a holiday in France, just visit this site.
http://sunsite.unc.edu/louvre
Rachel Prior, 11

Rock & Roll Hall of Fame and Museum

This site is for everyone who loves Rock 'n' Roll. It has lots of places to go, and the pictures are really stylish. You can even buy Rock'n' Roll merchandise and win prizes. You can also tour the museum and look at the exhibits or go backstage to the Rock'n' Roll Hall of Fame. This site gives you all the latest Rock'n' Roll news, too.
http://www.rockhall.com
David Reilly, 10

A Walking Tour of Plimoth Plantation

Plimoth Plantation is a living museum now, but a long time ago this was the first European settlement in New England. There are two parts to the museum. One is a reconstructed Pilgrim village and the other is a reconstructed Native American hamlet. The original settlement dates back to 1620!!! The Web site has links to pictures of all kinds of tools, storage, food, and houses used by the Pilgrims and the Indians centuries ago!!!!!! This is a great site if you'd like to be a time traveler or if you're doing a report for school!!!

http://spirit.lib.uconn.edu/ArchNet/Topical/Historic/Plimoth /Plimoth.html
David Sawchak, 7

Smithsonian Institution

This is one huge spot, covering all the Smithsonian places. Visit any of the many museums and learn about what can be seen there as well as its location, admission fees, hours it's open, special events, research projects, education activities, and new and temporary exhibits. Plan your visit from your home. Choose from such museums as the National Air and Space museum, National Museum of History, and the Postal Museum—the list goes on and on. In the National Zoo, you can find out about when animals are fed, what you shouldn't miss, new babies and additions, and check out the Animal Photo Library. There are even audio tours to take.

http://www.si.edu
Nykki-Lynn Smelser, 10

The History of Grunge

The term grunge evolved through word of mouth. As Nils Bernstein, of Sub Pop, recalls, "People here used the word tongue in cheek: 'It's kind of like dirty, scuzzy, grungy music.' 'What do you call it?' 'Oh, I don't know... grunge!'" Soundgarden and Mother Love Bone were the first of Seattle's alternative bands to sign with major record companies. In September 1991, the cornerstone albums of the Seattle scene—Pearl Jam's Ten and Nirvana's Nevermind—were released. Seattle then became a full-blown rock and roll capital. Bands from the still-vital Seattle scene continue to shape the future of rock & roll.

Rock and Roll Hall of Fame and Museum
http://www.rockhall.com

Virtual Tour

Who cares if you're grounded? Even if you can't leave the block, you can still take a trip around the world. Virtual tours are ready to go whenever you are

Dem Bones

Kenya is sometimes referred to as the "cradle of mankind" since the now famous digs of the Leaky family. Their finds included humanoid skulls dating back 2 million years. These discoveries radically altered theories about the origin of humankind.

World Surfari: Fun From Afar!
http://www.supersurf.com/fun.htm

World Surfari: Fun From Afar!

Every month, the World Surfari travels someplace new. In July, the World Surfari travelled to Kenya. On this page, you will find email from Kenya, information on customs of the Kenyans, and recipes for beef stew and pilau rice. Did you know Kenya has golf courses? Yes! A lot of them. The most amazing fact about this page is that it is made by a kid! You can even learn Swahili (the Kenyan language)! If you want to travel the world without moving from your chair, this is the place for you!!
http://www.supersurf.com/fun.htm
Jeff Little, 13

National Geographic Online

National Geographic Online is a wonderful place to explore for all. You can be a part of an interactive expedition like Ice Treasures of the Inca, or even help uncover a sunken ship. Whether you're reading about South Africa's parks or an account of a survivor of the *Titanic*, you're sure to learn as you explore.
http://www.nationalgeographic.com
Melissa Edwards, 14

Around the World in 80 Clicks

This is a launch site (a site that features links to many other sites) with links to places all over the world. Click on the map to find out about any place on earth. The dot on Washington, D.C. will take you to the White House home page. Take a tour of the Champs Elysees Virtuels by clicking on Paris. This is definitely the place to go if you're in the mood for some virtual traveling.

http://www.coolsite.com/arworld.html
Katie Tandler, 13

Virtual World Tours

This site is huge! You can visit the whole world, right from here! You can tour a country, or even a city in a different country, or visit a whole region if you want. There is also a virtual tour of the U.S. government. They have gorgeous pictures from all over. Bookmark this site for geography and social studies homework!

http://www.dreamscape.com/frankvad
Kelsey Mays, 11

Anatomy of a Rapid

"Running a rapid is an all-or-nothing proposition. Unlike tennis, there's no second serve. Unlike fishing, there's no reeling the line back in to try another cast. Shooting a white-water rapid requires that you get it right the first time.

There's the roar of the white water, the boat drifting slowly toward the drop, the seconds stretching until it seems as though they'll snap. The boat slides down into that strangely smooth section of water known as the tongue, a kind of calm before the storm. Then, the first wave. Your heart pounds, your fists clench, and you are in it: white water."

National Geographic: The River Wild
http://www.nationalgeo
graphic.com/modules
/selway/index.html

Chapter 7

The Den

i like the Internet because it gives me a chance to meet people from all over the world. It also gives me a place to find information on just about any subject. And it gives me a place to find things that are fun to do. I look at sites about my favorite bands, Green Day and The Presidents of the United States of America. I play games like The Realm. I'm building a BBS with tools from the Internet. I get information for school reports. I go to chat forums to meet people from all over the world (Australia is the farthest away so far.)

David Lindsay 11
CALGARY, CANADA

My Top Sites

1. **The Realm**
   http://www.realmserver.com

2. **Sid Meier's Civilization II**
   http://www.microprose.com/civll

3. **Awesome Cyber Cards Card Finder**
   http://www.marlo.com/cardfind.htm

4. **Redwall Abbey**
   http://www.islandnet.com/~qnd/redwall/homepage.html

5. **InfoSeek**
   http://guide.infoseek.com

Location: http://www.realmserver.com/

THE REALM

ABOUT THE REALM
DEVELOPING THE REALM
WHY YOU'LL PLAY THE REALM
Q&A ON THE REALM
CONTACTING THE DEVELOPERS
PREVIEW REALM ARTWORK

PLAYING THE REALM
WHAT YOU'LL NEED
REGISTERING FOR TEST VERSION
DOWNLOADING THE TEST VERSION
LINKS TO USER'S PERSONAL PAGE
README FILE
REALM INFORMATION SHEET

Board Games

Do you want a good reason for playing board games in cyberspace? Here's one—you never lose the pieces!

Monopoly

A nice, ruthless, money-hungry Web site. If you already own the CD-ROM game, you needn't visit this site, since it is mainly based around that game. You can play over the Internet with millions of people worldwide. If you don't have time to play the game, you could just sample the stunning 3-D graphics in a QuickTime or AVI movie, or just a still frame. If you are one of the minority of people who don't know the rules, you can read the rules page before beginning to play.
http://www.monopoly.com
Philip Reilly, 12

The WWW Backgammon Page

Attention all backgammon lovers, this page is definitely for you! It is filled with links on every single little detail about backgammon for the real backgammon nut! Anything that you could possibly want to know about backgammon, you will find right here! It's got more than the average person might want to know!
http://www.statslab.cam.ac.uk/`stretl/backgammon/main.html
Andrea Bonilla, 13

GET THIS!

Backgammon is one of the oldest games in existence, dating back at least 5,000 years!

Backgammon FAQ
http://www.cybercom.net
/~damish/backgammon
/bg-faq.html#what_is
_backgammon

The Risk Page

This page is all about the game of Risk. Here, you will find the rules book, different variations, tips and strategies, and more. If you like to play Risk, you should check out this site and all the cool stuff it has. The tips and strategies should help you play better.

http://www.macshack.com/johns/risk/risk.html
Erin Fleege, 13

Internet Chess Club

The Internet Chess Club is a group of industrious hobbyists who love to play chess. The ICC proudly tells the world, "Over 5,000 chess games played daily!" So, if you register to play chess over telnet with a member of the club, you can rest assured there will be plenty of competition. You can register as a guest for a seven-day trial, totally free, with all registered features. Your registration is processed, so you'll receive your password, etc. through email in a matter of minutes.

http://www.hydra.com/icc
David Lindsay, 11

Web Chess

If you enjoy playing "reality" chess, try your hand at "cyber-reality" chess! Now you can play chess against other people on the Web, or you can watch other games being played! The logo is very, very neat with 3-D graphics! This page also provides instructions for the game! This is a very kewl site.

http://www.williamette.edu/~tjones/chessmain.html
Alex Landback, 10

History of Chess

Chess is about 1,400 years old. It was invented in India, around the year 550. From there it moved east and west. The rules changed as it migrated. In China, it became a game known as xianqi, which is still played today. In Europe and the Middle East, it became chess. Over several hundred years, the Indians taught the game to the Persians, who taught it to the Arabs, who taught it to the Spaniards. Spaniards then taught the rest of Europe. The word chess comes from the Persian word for king, shah. Checkmate comes from the Persian for "the King is dead," shah mat.

History of Chess
http://www.sojourn.com
/~sean/web/cheshist.html

Video Games

Do the words Descent, Doom, Quake, and Crash Bandicoot make your hands twitch? Then you may be a video game addict. Take two of these sites and see how you feel in the morning

Enter Mortal Kombat

Enter Mortal Kombat has great graphics, video and audio clips and behind-the-scenes info. Someone has obviously put a lot of work into this site. This is THE site for Mortal Kombat fans.
http://www.directnet.com
Bronwyn Lee, 12

Marathon Central

This is the central source (hence the name) for Marathon information on the Internet. (I'm talking about the game, not the twenty-six mile run.) From this site you should be able to access all the Marathon info under the sun. If it's not on this site, you can find it on one of the many Marathon links. There is also a Marathon Map of the Month page, where you can send your Marathon map, or just look at somcone else's. A great site for computer game lovers.
http://www.marathon.org
Philip Reilly, 12

GET THIS!

You can vote for your favorite all-time video games. These were the Segasages Top 5 games from September 26, 1996. 296 people voted.

1 Tekken 2 PSX
2 Nights SAT
3 Resident Evil PSX
4 Mario 64 N64
5 Virtua Fighter 2 SAT
http://www.segasages.com /top100

Nintendo (on AOL)

This is one of the best areas online for kids interested in video games. Whether you are new or old to the exciting world of Nintendo, there is something for everyone. Nintendo has its own chat room and message boards, too, so you can discuss things and make new friends. Games is one of the best features. It include sneak previews of upcoming Nintendo products. Systems is another good feature.

America Online Go Nintendo
Kelly Roman, 11

Sega Online

Sega just overwhelms you with information on their site. Some categories include: Sega channel, Sega gameworks, Sega entertainment, Segasoft, Sega foundation, and the latest news at Sega. Unbelievable graphics are another great thing about the site. You can even chat to other Sega users or search for Sega games. There are even contests to enter and win! An A+++ site!

http://www.sega.com
Jeff Little, 13

Sony Playstation Home Page

If you own a Sony Playstation, this page has got tons of stuff for you. It's got newsflashes, promotion and other information. The Arena contains info on almost all the games currently available, info on all the upcoming games and games categories. A good site, but it could be bigger and better.

http://www.scea.sony.com/SCEA
Philip Reilly, 12

Nostalgia Corner

Do your older relatives get sof-headed and nostalgia about old games systems like ColecoVision? Find out what they're talking about and download a version you can play on your PC.

Video Game Graveyard
http://www.cyberhighway
.net/~bfetter/gravel.html

Barbie

Barbie made her debut at the American Toy Fair in New York City in February, 1959. For a middle-aged woman she's looking pretty good these days

Barbie Gets Respect

In the early seventies, when many women were fighting for equal rights with men, Barbie changed too. She became more movable than ever, and was given fringe-trimmed and tie-dyed outfits. In early versions of Barbie, she always looks to the side, never right at you. This body language was thought to mean that she was content to be a second-class citizen. In 1971, she began to look straight back.

Barbie: The Image of Us All
http://darwin.clas.virginia.edu/~tsawyer/barbie/barb.html

Barbie: The Image of Us All

This page looks boring, but the links on it lead to interesting places. Find out how Barbie was invented, what Barbie looked like in the '60s, '70s, '80s and '90s. There is lots of information to read. Find out about the problems Ken caused and the full history of Barbie. This is a cool page for Barbie fans. You can even leave comments or suggestions. There are going to be changes to Barbie. If you want to know what the changes are, what are you waiting for? Look at the site.
http://darwin.clas.virginia.edu/~tsawyer/barbie/barb.html
Danielle Jacovelli, 11

Barbie Hall of Fame

This has lots of information on how Barbie began, what Barbies have been created, and the creator of Barbie. This is really for kids. It contains no games or really anything to do but read. This site could use work, but all in all it's a good site to read about Barbie.

http://sunsite.unc.edu/stayfree/11/barbie.htm

Beth Yankee, 11

Annette on the Net

Annette on the Net, is a web page designed and maintained by an artist in England who collects and "refinishes" old Barbie and Barbie-like dolls. If you are a fan of any doll, especially Barbie, take a look at this marvelous idea that Annette has created. She starts with old dolls and turns them into works of art. Inspired by classic Indian dances, the dolls are absolutly unique in every way you could imagine. The only thing you might have against the site is the lay-out. The webmaster should have acknowledged just exactly what the dolls are, and how they are made, rather than making the reader search. Check this site out, you are sure to want to drag your dolls out and play with them again!!

http://dspace.dial.pipex.com/town/square/fj09/dolls.html

Kellie Vaughn, 13

Trivia

Q: What doll was the original Barbie modelled after?

A: A German doll named Lilli.

Q: What year did Barbie meet Ken on the toy shelves?

A: 1961.

Barbie: The Image of Us All
http://darwin.clas.virginia.edu/~tsawyer/barbie/barb.html

Puzzles

If your forefinger is getting sore from zapping aliens with your mouse, maybe it's time to find a new kind of computer fun. Use the portable variety—your brain

Very Punny!

A boy was bagging groceries at a supermarket. One day the store installed a machine for squeezing fresh orange juice. Intrigued, the young man asked if he could be allowed to work the machine, but his request was denied. Said the store manager, "Sorry, kid, but baggers can't be juicers."

What do you get when you throw a grenade into a kitchen in France? Linoleum blown apart.

Chet Meeks' Page of Puns
http://www.ccinet.ab.ca /city-of-gp/puns.htm

Puzzle Archives

This page was very interesting. It has questions about physics, language, logic, and even cryptology. This page is very educational. There were no graphics or even a background, but it got right to the point.
http://www.nova.edu/Inter-Links/puzzles.html
Emily Malloch, 11

Slide puzzles

If you're the kind of person who loves a good puzzle every once in a while, this site is a good place to go. It features one of those classic nine-piece slide puzzles that you can play right from the site. The puzzle seems simple, but it can drive you crazy! Here's a tip: Bookmark the page so if you get frustated, take a break, do something else, maybe browse a few other sites. Then, when you come back to the site, you might figure out how to solve it more easily.
http://www.bu.edu/games/puzzle (Slide puzzle)
Katie Tandler, 13

John's Word Search Puzzles

If you are bored and alone and you like word puzzles, then this is the perfect site for YOU! It has word search puzzles of all kinds! Here are some examples: Inventors, Antique Cars, Bible New Testament, Bible Old Testament, Space, Candy, Computer Stuff, etc. etc. etc! You can print these out and have a GREAT time doing them while your mom or dad are surfing the Internet (or working on the PC)!

http://www.neosoft.com/~jrpotter/puzzles.html
David Sawchak, 7

Math Magic Activities

Well, this page is kind of boring, but it gives you some neat info on how to do a few magic tricks. It tells you how to do some card tricks, calculator tricks, and geometry- and topology-based magic tricks. It was all based on math. If you like math, this page is for you.

http://www.scri.fsu.edu/~dennisl/topics/math_magic.html
Emily Malloch, 11

The Magic Calculator

In this trick you will pretend to be able to see through a calculator. Get a friend to do this:

1. Enter any number that is easy to remember in the calculator without letting you see it. Tell them to make sure that the number has less than 8 digits.
2. Multiply that number by 3.
3. Add 45 to that answer.
4. Multiply that answer by 2.
5. Divide that answer by 6.
6. Subtract their original number from the previous result.
7. Finally tell your friend to hold the back of the calculator towards you. Pretend you can read through solid objects and then state that the number in the display is 15! It always will be!

Math Magic Activities
http://www.scri.fsu.edu
/~dennisl/topics/math
_magic.html

Toys

Have you ever wanted some toy you saw on TV so badly you couldn't stand it? And then you got it. And it was rubbish. Don't believe the hype! Try online before you buy!

Q: How many different ways are there to put Legos together?

A: There are 102,981,500 ways to put together six 8-stud bricks—and that's if they're all the same color.

The LEGO World Wide Web
http://www.LEGO.com

Dr. Toy

This page is great for parents and kids. It has great tips on which toys you should get for your kids, the 100 best children's awards, links to other fun pages, and some really neat contests for kids. If you're a grown up who is trying to decide on a toy for your kid, or just a kid looking for some fun, this page is the place to be.
http://www.drtoy.com/drtoy/index.html
Emily Malloch, 11

Life Before Nintendo

There aren't any toys surviving from the time of cave dwellers, but the ancient Egyptians did leave some dolls, rattles, toy animals, tops and game boards. The Greeks and Romans left descriptions of lots of different toys, including rag dolls, pull-cars and even yo-yos!

Historical Toys
http://museon.museon.nl/objextra.eng
/historis.html

R.aving T.oy M.aniac Page

COOL KID SITE

If you really love toys, this is the page for you! This page gives you plenty of types of the toys you are looking for! For example, some links he has listed are Lego, X-Men, action figures, etc. You witness some pretty neat graphics! Everything else is toy-rrific!!
http://utmdacc.mda.uth.tmc.edu:5014
/eric/rtm/rtm.html
Alex Landback, 10

The Toy Closet

The Toy Closet is all about toys! Right now, the Toy Closet has links to toy sites and a few paragraphs about toys, but in the future, it will probably be a big toy site. Put a bookmark to it, and take a look a month or so later, and you'll probably find what you're looking for.

http://euclid.barry.edu/~gordon/toys.htm

Erin Fleege, 13

The Official LEGO World Wide Web

This site has everything a pro Lego builder needs to know! There's a membership club, cool membership offers, and Lego news! This site has really cool animated pictures on the home page. You can even make your own Lego home page of personal best links. Your Lego home page has a couple of links already built in, including a link to a Download Zone where you can download little movies, a screen saver, and other cool stuff, too.

http://www.lego.com

David Sawchak, 7

Zarf's Interactive Games

Zarf's has some pretty good games and toys on it. Parents should check out some of the games before letting their kids play them because there are a few that are not very appropriate for kids. You also have to watch out because some of them cost money.

http://www.leftfoot.com/realgames.html

Andrea Bonilla, 13

The Lego Legend

Legos were invented by a Danish toymaking company named Lego. The word Lego is short for *leg godt*, Danish words that mean "play well." The company's first plastic bricks were made in 1949. Now 9,000 people working in 50 countries make Legos. The Lego company estimates that nearly 300 million kids and adults play or have played with Legos. Every year, kids worldwide spend more than 5 billion hours playing with those amazing plastic bricks.

The LEGO World Wide Web
http://www.lego.com

The Library

If you're looking for a good book, if you're trying to find out something about one of your favorite books, or you want to publish one of your own stories, read up on it online

Alice's Adventures in Wonderland

The complete text of this great children's story by Lewis Carroll is here. It is sort of convenient because you don't have to go to the trouble of finding the book, you can just read it on the Net. It's also fun because there are full color pictures of the characters, like in the real book. The story is divided into 12 chapters so if you get tired at the end of one chapter you can easily come back later and continue! Forgot what happened? Press the "previous button" to go back. When you've finished reading the chapter simply press the "forward button" to move to the next chapter. This is the next best thing to curling up in bed with the real book!
http://www.cstone.net/library/alice/aliceinwonderland.html
Derya Davenport, 11

Anne Frank Remembered

This is a great place to find out about the girl whose diary is one of the most read worldwide, Anne Frank. Find out what life was like for the girl some call Hitler's best-known victim. Read about the Holocaust and visit the Holocaust Memorial

Museum. While here, check out the text files, images, video and sounds clips of World War II. It is important we learn from history so as not to repeat past mistakes.

http://www.spe.sony.com/Pictures/SonyClassics/annefrank

Nykki-Lynn Smelser, 10

The ROALD DAHL Index

This is definitely an extremely fun site for kids. If you are a Roald Dahl fan, this is a must see. Lia, the host of the site, even has a biweekly recipe for you to read from Roald Dahl's Revolting Recipes. There are links to other Roald Dahl pages, information on the books and even information on future movies. Overall, come and have a ball!

http://www.tridel.com.ph/user/bula/rdahl.htm

Kelly Roman, 11

Diary of a Young Girl

One of the best books about the Holocaust was written by a girl named Anne Frank. The Holocaust is the name given to the Nazis' attempt to kill all Jewish people during World War II. Anne and her family spent more than two years hiding in the small rooms above her father's offices in Amsterdam. After being betrayed to the Nazis, the Frank family was arrested and deported to Nazi concentration camps. Nine months later, Anne died of typhus at the Bergen-Belsen camp. She was 15 years old. Her diary was first published in 1947. It's one of the most widely read books in the world, and has been translated into 55 languages.

Anne Frank Remembered

http://www.spe.sony.com /Pictures/SonyClassics /annefrank

Advice from Dr. Seuss

Theodore Geisel, the writer we know as Dr. Seuss, was once asked by Dartmouth College to give a graduation speech. This is what he said:

"My Uncle Terwilliger on the Art of Eating Popovers"
My uncle ordered popovers
from the restaurant's bill of fare.
And when they were served,
he regarded them
with a penetrating stare.
Then he spoke great Words of Wisdom
as he sat there on that chair:
"To eat these things,"
said my uncle,
"you must exercise great care.
You may swallow down what's solid...
BUT
you must spit out the air!"
And...
as you partake of the world's bill of fare,
That's darned good advice to follow.
Do a lot of spitting out the hot air
And be careful what you swallow.

CyberSeuss
http://www.afn.org/~afn1530l/drseuss.html

The Dr. Seuss Page

Every person in the country can identify with one book—*Dr. Seuss's The Cat in the Hat*. Nobody can deny that they have heard this story at least once in their kindergarten years, and most can also identify two or three other Seuss books as well. This site has a list of books and movies, a biography, and a few parodies of Dr. Seuss books, too. This site isn't too flashy, but it's got lots of info, and the parodies are fantastically funny.
http://klinzhai.iuma.com/~drseuss/seuss
Katie Tandler, 13

The Madeleine L'Engle Fan Homepage

This Madeleine L'Engle Fan Homepage was under construction when reviewed with a message of more to come. Madeleine L'Engle is the author of many children's fiction books (including *The Twenty-Four Days Before Christmas*, *The Young Unicorns*, and *A Wrinkle in Time*). You can view a list of some of her other children's and adult novels. As there are no graphics, unless you're interested in the list of books, you may not find this spot worth a visit.
http://wwwvms.utexas.edu/~eithlan/lengle.html
Nykki-Lynn Smelser, 10

Goosebumps

The greatest thing about this site is all the cool Java and animation. The Goosebumps sign drips blood and a spider crawls across the screen. There is information on the author, TV series, the history of Goosebumps, and a list of books by the author. Also included is a photo gallery with pictures from the TV series. A very informative site!

http://www.scholastic.com/public/Goosebumps /Cover.html

Jeff Little, 13

Goosebumps-0

The Goosebumps page is bloody and slimy with bugs that can lead you to horror! The show comes on on Friday at 4:30. Watch it if you dare. You can see pictures of a guy who turns into his dog every night, and a spooky dummy that talks by itself. You can read about what the books are about before you go off and buy them for no reason! If you like what the story is about, you can buy that book. Don't read them or look at the Goosebumps page on your computer screen at night, because you might get spooky dreams.

http://scholastic.com/Goosebumps /index.html

Susanna Wolff, 8

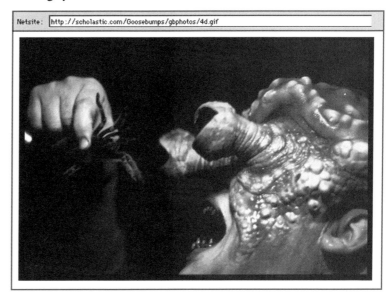

Netsite: http://scholastic.com/Goosebumps/gbphotos/4d.gif

The Real Christopher Robin

Did you know there was a real Christopher Robin? His father, A.A. Milne, wrote the stories. Christopher Robin Milne spent most of his life running a book-shop in Dartmouth, England.

The Author of Winnie-the-Pooh

http://www.public.iastate .edu/~jmilne/pooh/milne .html#top

My Little House on the Prairie Home Page

For anyone who's ever seen any episode of this classic series, this site is interesting: a very large, colorful page with all the info on the Ingalls, the book series, merchandise, links and more! You can read about every book about the Prairie folk, and read about all the characters. A great source for any fan with loads of information, coming attractions and fan links. Even if you've never seen the series, it's still a worthwhile visit.
http://www.vvv.com/~jenslegg
Hayley Morgan, 12

The Pooh Pages: A Winnie the Pooh Exposition

This hunny of a page is really fun! It's especially Tigger-rific if you're a Pooh fan, but you don't have to be to have lots of fun here! You can get recipes at the Piknik Place, go to lots of other Pooh pages, take a look at some pictures, see what other people think of the Pooh Pages at Pooh's Thotful Page, and quite a bit more! It's a Roo-eally exciting "expotition"!
http://worldaccess.com/pooh /welcome.html
Sarah Alderdice, 10

Sweet Valley Intro

Sweet Valley Intro is a great place for people who enjoy the Sweet Valley books. You'll find information on *Sweet Valley Kids*, *Sweet Valley Twins*, *Sweet Valley High* and *Sweet Valley University*. One of the best parts is the Book Review section. You'll know which books to look for. The best part is that you can check off which books you have read!

http://w3.one.net/~voyager/sv.html

Kelly Roman, 11

Location: http://w3.one.net/~voyager/sv.html

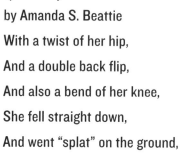

Bad Aim Dive (Poem)

by Amanda S. Beattie

With a twist of her hip,

And a double back flip,

And also a bend of her knee,

She fell straight down,

And went "splat" on the ground,

For terrible aim had she.

KidPub

http://www.en-garde
.com/kidpub

The Young Writers Club

Extra, extra, read all about it! The Young Writers Club (TYWC) is on the Internet! The cool-looking background invites you into the site, and you know exactly where you are because the site explains all that at the beginning. Feel free to link to About TYWC, Storybooks, Activities, and many more! The site tells about each link. So get your pencils ready for The Young Writers Club!

http://www.cs.bilkent.edu.tr/~david/derya/ywc.html

Morgan Balavage, 12

Chapter

8 The Dark Side

i think the Web is a great place to learn, but... it's really great for fun too! I think the most frustrating part about the Web is when pages load really slowly. The Net is great for research on reports that you have to do for school. I like to look for my favorite television shows on the Web. I think kids just getting started will find that the Web is a whole new world where you control what you see. Some advice though: stay away from the ADULT pages and also do not give out personal information on the Web.

Emily Malloch 11

NEW BERLIN, NEW YORK, USA

My Top Sites

1. **The Official X-Files Page**
   http://www.thex-files.com

2. **All the unofficial X-Files pages**

3. **Ralph's home page**
   http://www.norwich.net/~mallochr/ralph.htm

4. **The Emily Zone**
   http://www.norwich.net/~mallochr/emily.htm

Location: http://www.thex-files.com/

Aliens & UFOs

We are either alone in the universe or not. Both ideas are overwhelming
—Arthur C. Clarke

July 4 Forever

COOL KID SITE

You probably saw the film *Indendence Day*, but if that wasn't enough you can join in the fight against gruesome aliens at this great fun site!

Independence Day
http://www.id4.com

UFOs & E.T.s

This is a really cool Web site filled with lots of information on UFOs and E.T.s. You can read people's accounts of when they saw a UFO or alien. They also have tons of pictures of UFOs and a few of aliens that people have seen. They have info on Greys, too, and much more. If you are interested in learning about UFOs and stuff like that, you should definitely visit this site.

http://www.io.org/~dnewton/ufo.html
Alexandra Barsk, 12

Pleiades Index

If you are interested in UFOs, then this site is an absolute must see. If you're into astronomy, this place is definitely great. If you're into astrology, this page is terrific. If you're into SEISMOLOGY, this place is cool. It has TONS of info on UFOs, star stuff, etc. Even if you're not a big fan of these topics, this page is pretty neat. You're almost sure to find something here.

http://www.powertech.no/~pleiades
Sarah Alderdice, 10

Alien Exploratorium

The Alien Exploratorium is pretty freaky... and at the same time, really cool. Did you know that there may have been a human skeleton on the moon when Apollo 11 landed there? That's just one of the things you might find information on at The Alien Exploratorium. This site has many, many articles on all kinds of alien things, ranging from UFO sightings and alien autopsies, to abductions and Walt Disney World's Alien Encounter ride. You can also browse through some alien pictures. Everything in this site is very weird; some may be considered offensive, so don't read it if you can't stand this sort of stuff!

http://area51.upsu.plym.ac.uk/~moosie/ufo/aexplo.htm

Erin Fleege, 13

The Roswell Incident

In the most well-known UFO case, the Roswell Incident, an object crashed in a remote location on a large ranch in New Mexico in 1947. Debris was recovered by U.S. Air Force officials, who issued a hasty press release saying a "flying disk" had been recovered. The press release was retracted the next day and sources stated the object was a device used to adjust radar. But 30 years later, an Air Force intelligence officer claimed that the object was "not of this earth" and that the press conference was a sham. Could aliens and their spacecraft be making visits to our planet? Fifty percent of Americans think so.

Internet UFO Group
http://www.iufog.org

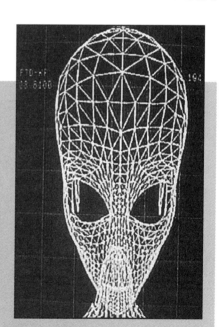

Horror Movies

Greetings, mortal. Welcome to the Internet's chamber of horrors. Ghosts, witches, vampires, and monsters— we're all here, waiting for you to visit us. If you dare...

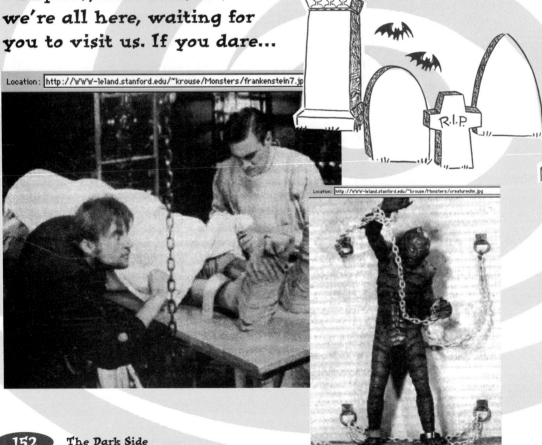

Location: http://WWW-leland.stanford.edu/~krouse/Monsters/frankenstein7.jp

Location: http://WWW-leland.stanford.edu/~krouse/Monsters/creaturehn.jpg

R.I.P.

Horror In The Movies

This page is great for every single person who has ever watched a horror movie. Besides having a really neat background it also has clips of horror movies, a list of actors and directors that have made horror movies, most-recommended horror films, and a horror movie reference guide. It even has some horror movie FAQs. If you think horror movies are too scary, don't worry.

http://www.rat.pdx.edu/~caseyh/
horror/movie.html

Emily Malloch, 11

The Woman Who Invented Frankenstein

Mary Shelley wrote *Frankenstein*, the book all the movies have been based on, when she was only 19! She started it on a dare in the summer of 1816, while staying with poet Percy Shelley and their other writer friends at a villa in Switzerland. The poet Lord Byron had challenged everyone to write a ghost story. Byron wrote a vampire story, but everyone else had a hard time. The poets gave up, but Mary Shelley persisted. She went to bed and had a vision of a monster coming to life. The next morning, she began to write.

The Life of Mary Shelley

http://www.netaxs.com/~kwbridge/life.html

Unexplained Phenomena

Bigfoot, the Bermuda Triangle, the Loch Ness Monster... what's real? What's not? Take a look at the evidence on the Net

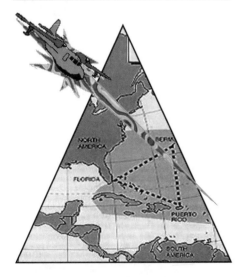

GET THIS!

Even today, the U.S. Navy has a standing order for crews to keep a look out for Flight 19 which disappeared in the Bermuda Triangle.

The Bermuda Triangle
http://tigger.cc.uic.edu /~toby-g/tri.html

Nessie on the Net

This is a very organized page on the controversial subject of the Loch Ness Monster. It claims that the pictures shown on its page are genuine photographs of Nessie. It also contains a database of sightings. And you can vote on whether to put up a parking lot or a restaurant nearby, or leave it alone. It's a pretty good page.
http://www.scotnet.co.uk/highland/index.html
Emily Malloch, 11

The Bermuda Triangle

Did you ever wonder if the Bermuda Triangle stories are true? This site tells about weird experiences in the Bermuda Triangle, and then tells the facts. This site is really awesome to look at. Even if you're not into the Bermuda Triangle, you will find yourself getting more and more interested once you start reading. The cloudy background makes you feel like you're actually in the Triangle. The Bermuda Triangle Web site is definitely a cool site to check out.
http://tigger.cc.uic.edu/~toby-g/tri.html
Erin Fleege, 13

The Bigfoot Research Project

This is probably the most informative Bigfoot page on the entire Net. It shows research procedures, what is known about him to date, evidence of his existence, how to contribute to the research, and a few links to other Bigfoot sites. The site is very well organized; there aren't too many pictures to load. People who are into Bigfoot will definitely love this page.
http://www.teleport.com/~tbrp
Katie Tandler, 13

The Unsolved Mysteries Page

Get information and photographs of lost loves, missing people, wanted fugitives, and a special bulletin from previous *Unsolved Mysteries* shows. Can you identify anyone in the Gallery of Fugitives? This site is updated weekly, and they will also be including cases that haven't been on TV yet. Maybe YOU can help solve a mystery.
http://www.unsolved.com
Nykki-Lynn Smelser, 10

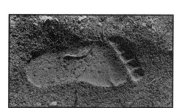

A Bigfoot By Any Other Name

Bigfoot, Sasquatch, the Abominable Snowman—there are more than 50 names for the large, bipedal, hair-covered hominid (translation: big, hairy ape-man) who has supposedly been spotted in woody areas around the world. This woolly wonder is known as Yeti in Tibet, and Yowie in Australia. In Scotland, they call 'em as they see 'em—he's the Big Gray Man. In Arkansas, he's been referred to as the Wild Man of the Woods. Theodore Roosevelt called the creature the Snow Walker. But perhaps the most appropriate nickname comes from the Lake Iliamna Athabascan Indians of Alaska—they simply call him Get Gun.

The Bigfoot Research Project
http://www.teleport
.com/~tbrp

Chapter 9 : The Way of the Web

What I like about the Internet is that I can look up stuff that I need; I can get sports scores, stock prices (I own a couple), and just have fun! What makes me frustrated about the Internet is when it takes forever to download sounds, pictures, etc. Another thing that makes me frustrated is when I log on to the Internet. That is because we have friends who started a server called Propeller Head. This is brand new, so it has some problems in the system. One problem I have with most kids pages is that adults write them, and most are "not so good" pages. They aren't really "kids' pages."

Alex
Landback 10
TAMPA, FLORIDA, USA

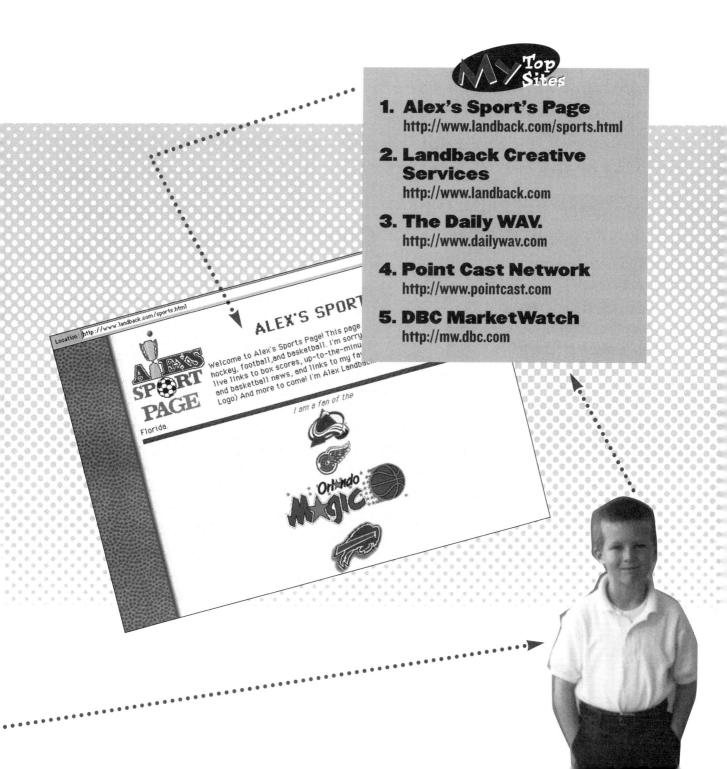

My Top Sites

1. **Alex's Sport's Page**
   http://www.landback.com/sports.html

2. **Landback Creative Services**
   http://www.landback.com

3. **The Daily WAV.**
   http://www.dailywav.com

4. **Point Cast Network**
   http://www.pointcast.com

5. **DBC MarketWatch**
   http://mw.dbc.com

ALEX'S SPORT PAGE

Location: http://www.landback.com/sports.html

ALEX'S SPORT

Welcome to Alex's Sports Page! This page
hockey, football, and basketball. I'm sorry
live links to box scores, up-to-the-minu
and basketball news, and links to my fav
Logo) And more to come! I'm Alex Landba

Florida.

I am a fan of the

Hubsites

Where do you go if you don't know exactly where you want to go? One of the best choices is to go to a hubsite

Sam's Free Stuff Page

If you're one of those types of people who like to get free stuff without any effort on your part, you'll probably like Sam's Free Stuff Page. On it you will find a wide variety of free things like jelly beans, CD-ROMS, Bumper Stickers, and even a free chocolate bar. Just about anyone will spend **HOURS** on this site getting as many free things as they wish. Hope your mailperson doesn't get mad!

http://www.thezone.pair .com/freestuff

Ian Grant, 14

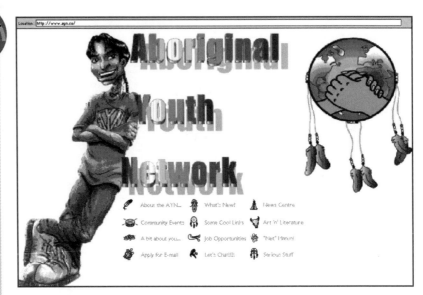

Aboriginal Youth Network

For those of you who do not know much about the Aboriginal Youth Network, it is groups of young Native Americans who are united by this club... Once you see this site, you will be ashamed if you have not stopped by before. From this page you can chat real-time, discover art and more native American history, or just learn a little more about the Aboriginal Youth Network.

http://www.ayn.ca

Kellie Vaughn, 13

Deaf CyberKids

This is not, as it may seem, just a site about deaf kids. It is a terrific site for any kid who likes to have fun (which of course everybody does). There are just too many wonderful places to go, a kid could get lost in all the kids sites here. It's especially terrific if you want to learn about deaf kids or if you are deaf, but also if you just want to go somewhere fun.
http://deafworldweb.org/dww/kids
Sarah Alderdice, 10

Youth Central

At this great site for youth and teens, there is quite a lot to do, as it is quite extensive. There are places to meet pen pals, learn about new subjects, and look at other kids' art and stories. You need the correct file types and plug-ins to see them, though.
http://www.youthcentral.apple.com
Hayley Morgan. 12

Her Online

By far the best place for girls on the Internet! You can talk to other girls online at the pizza place, check out the hot links, educational and school section, shopping and fashion, books and book reviews, entertainment, beauty and looks, art, sports, and music! This is a wonderful place for girls of around 10–18 that inspires the imagination and proves very interesting!
http://www.her-online.com
Hayley Morgan, 12

Why was the beach so strong?
Because it was full of mussels.

Magic School Bus Riddle of the Week
http://scholastic.com /MagicSchoolBus/games /riddle.html

What's gray and has four legs and a trunk?
A mouse on vacation.

Blackberry Creek
AOL Keyword: Blackberry

Location: http://www.her-online.com/room.html
Welcome to Your Room on Her Online

Location: http://www.michaels.com/kids/kid-main.html

Michaels THE ARTS AND CRAFTS STORE

KIDS CLUB!

Here's the place to find it all! Michaels Just for Kids Projects, the Kids Club Online Newsletter and a whole lot more! Be sure to come back soon and see what else we've added!

★Kids Club Project of the Month★

Brown Paper Scarecrow

KIDS CLUB online newsletter

Michael's Kids Club Online

Ideas, tips, projects, and fun for most ages can be found at Michael's. Visit the Project of the Week, which details a new craft each week, or go to Project Pages to find out about a bunch of other projects from previous weeks. There are even neat recipes kids can try... with adult supervision for the younger ones, of course. Write stories, solve puzzles, read about how spring is celebrated in other parts of world, and more. Hey, you can even surprise a friend on the Internet with a greeting card (Internote) right here.
http://www.michaels.com/kids/kid-main.html
Nykki-Lynn Smelser, 10

CyberKids

When you first arrive you will have the option of touring various linked sites throughout the CyberKids site. CyberKids is an online magazine for kids of any age who feel they would like to express their feelings through words, sounds, or art. CyberKids Space is a collection of artwork, poetry, and most recently added, music, from kids all over the world. You can even submit your recent creations to be displayed along with the others. Some of the great links that might interest you are: science, sports, museums and libraries, music, online books, and businesses. Anyone who is surfing the Net should stop by and take a look at this marvelous creation!
http://www.mtlake.com/cyberkids/CyberKidsIssues.html
Kellie Vaughn, 13

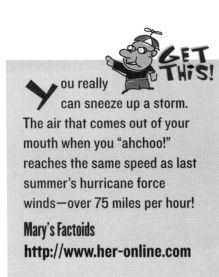

GET THiS!

You really can sneeze up a storm. The air that comes out of your mouth when you "ahchoo!" reaches the same speed as last summer's hurricane force winds—over 75 miles per hour!

Mary's Factoids
http://www.her-online.com

Magic School Bus Fun Place

WaHOO!!!!! Scholastic's Magic School Bus is on the Internet!!! It has a coloring book, riddle of the week, a store, a name word search game, kids' art, a television guide for *The Magic School Bus*, and more!! Plus, you can check the schedule to see if the bus is coming to you, LIVE and in person!
http://scholastic.com/MagicSchoolBus/index.html
David Sawchak, 7

Blackberry Creek

Got a case of the "Reads" (can't stop reading)? Then Blackberry Creek is the place for you! From chatting to getting your work published, Blackberry Creek has everything! In the Clubhouse, you can become a Creekie, read kids' newsletters, and so much more it's not even funny! There are two message boards for your reading pleasure. Among them are the Kids' Hangout and Story-Tellers Board. They call the chat room "Hungry Ear" and you can play online games or chat about various things. The Pixels is all about kids' artwork. Party People has fun suggestions for things to do at parties. Story Tellers is where you can read stories and poems. The Players has things such as movie reviews and plays by kids. The Best by Blackberry Creek are all the best plays, artwork, etc. kids have sent in. To send it in, go to Send Us Your Stuff.
America Online Keyword: Blackberry
Morgan Balavage, 12

Remembering Jessica Dubroff

Amid all the discussion about whether she should have flown at all cross-country from Half Moon Bay, or the incredible sadness over the tragic result of her take-off during a storm at Cheyenne, little Jessica remains every bit a heroine. This bright-eyed, smiling 7-year-old, we'll always picture with her flight jacket and baseball cap, was raised on the peace ideals of Mahatma Ghandi and Dr. Martin Luther King. But, most of all, what Jessica believed was that all of us, kids and adults, can aspire to be anything we can dream of being.

Kids in the Newz
http://www.azc.com/client/enn2/kidsnews.htm

Key pals

The Internet is a great place to make new friends. With email and chat programs you can meet people and talk to them straight away. And if you don't like them, switch them off!

Amber's Place—Girls Only!

This is for girls only. Amber lists all the girls-only clubs she has joined on the World Wide Web, gives a bit of information about them, and then provides little pictures underneath the info that you can click on to get more information on the club. It's pretty good if you're a club-crazy girl. If you're a boy, don't even try it!
http://www.davelash.com/amber/girlpage.html
Samantha Lipton, 12

Pen Pal List for Sarah Charlton's Entertainment Page

If you are looking for a pen pal, here's the place to go. Sarah has adult, teenager, and kid lists. There are heaps of people to choose from and each person has written a little about themselves. Why pay for a stamp and look everywhere for an envelope when you can email them? Write to anyone who comes from anywhere. Establish friends throughout the world. Encourage international peace and friendship.
http://www.islandnet.com/~bedford/s-pals.html
Rachel Prior, 11

Kid's Key Pal list

Marianne has a great page right here. In her page she has a list of countries to choose from. You'll find Australia, Canada, Japan, England, USA, and a couple of others. If you need a key pal you can place an ad or write to someone on the list. New friends are easily found!!
http://www.vir.com/~lubenskyi/keylist.htm
Rachel Prior, 11

The Electric Postcard

This is a great site to make your little notes, cheerios, or messages just a bit more interesting. The Electric Post Office offers you a large assortment of pics to use to send an email post card. Pick from paintings, photos, graphics, science, or cartoons. The Post Office provides you with simple instructions and before you know it, the postcard and your personal message will be sent. Great for beginners.
http://postcards.www.media.mit.edu/Postcards
Rachel Prior, 11

International Kid's Space

One of the coolest sites on the whole Web! It is a great place to find key pals and post links to your home page or see other kids' home pages. They also have lots of cool pictures and stories that are done by kids. To see it all, follow Guide Bear the first time you go here!
http://plaza.interport.net/kids_space
Kelsey Mays, 11

The Palace

This is the best chat program there is on the Net. You can talk to people as if you were there, and there are lots of rooms with interesting graphics. You can have a private conversation, or find the most crowded room there is. It's especially good for kids because it gives them a chance to meet other people and even some kids. But Palace does have a down side. It takes an hour to download, you have to pay $25 if you want member privileges (it's worth it), and it often gets very crowded, causing people to have "lag" and take forever to move or speak. Of course, this is still absolutely wonderful. If you do one thing on the Internet, let this be it. It's really terrific.
http://www.thepalace.com
Sarah Alderdice, 10

Chat Room Links

This site has a nice selection of links to various chat rooms, most of which don't require any special applications like IRC- or Java-capable browsers, but there are two or three that do. These links will satisfy all tastes, whether you like sports or *Star Wars*, *X-Files*, or *Earth 2*, or if you just want to chat about no particular topic at all. Anyone who likes to chat or wants to start out should visit here.
http://www.drsystems.com/chatLink.html
Katie Tandler, 13

Webchat

This is a Web site that lets you chat over the World Wide Web. It is harder to use and slower than IRC-chatting, but you can do cool stuff like link to your home page or email address and use a picture from your home page. There are chat rooms for all age groups from pre-teen and up.
http://wbs.net/cgi-bin/wbs/tune.cgi
Kelsey Mays, 11

Scholastic (on AOL)

This Web site allows you to go to different topics, the best one being Kids' World. From here you can go to different topics you would like to read about, such as sports, music, or movies. If you want to you can include your own opinion in the list of comments that other

kids have posted. This isn't very interesting in some ways— it isn't very active for one thing—but otherwise it's pretty fun.
America Online Keyword: scholastic
Alexandra Barsk, 12

Magazines

At every newstand and in every bookstore there are thousands of magazines about every subject under the sun. The Net is just the same, and some mags are just for kids

GET THIS!

A submersible, called Alvin, was used to recover a hydrogen bomb accidentally dropped from an air force bomber back in 1966.

YES Mag for Kids
http://www.islandnet.com /~yesmag/submarine.html

Location: http://www.pleasantco.com/ag/ag.cgi

★American Girl★ Celebrating Girls, Yesterday and Today.

Make Your Own Fortune!

READ ALL ABOUT IT
New! Try the Scavenger Hunt

ToDo Today
New Ideas Every Day!

HELP FROM YOU
Always picked last

You Said It
Cause for Alarms!

American Girl

I love it because it is very interesting. My favorite club is Wiggly Worm Watchers because it is about babysitters. It is simple and colorful and easy to get around on. This is a site to go back to over and over again. There is good stuff to do here. I liked it enough to make it one of my bookmarks, and it left me wanting to come back.
http://www.pleasantco.com
Amy Schroeder, 10

KidPub WWW

For starters, this page will delight any literature fan in the house! This site uses the stories and poems of kids to open the minds of others. The page is definitely kid - approved, judging by the number of works submitted— over 4,000!! The site recognizes the literary abilities of children by selecting a poem for the KidPub Publisher's Picks. This terrific site has also won several awards for its outstanding design. Stop by and take a look!!
http://www.en-garde.com/kidpub
Kellie Vaughn, 13

Kidworld

Kidworld is an Internet magazine for kids age 16 and under. It has news, comics (which your parents might like), puzzles, letters to "Dear Ashley," and more! If you write stories or draw pictures, you can send them in and Kidworld will put them on the Internet. It has a link to the official SafeSurf WWW site. You can find a pen pal there, too!

http://www.bconnex.net/~kidworld

David Sawchak, 7

Street Cents Online

If you're tired of getting ripped off, then you should check out this page! This is an award-winning Canadian TV show that helps make kids better consumers. Kids can send in their beefs by email, and every week they talk about different products that kids buy, like hockey sticks, comic books, sneakers, and lots more. There is lots of useful online information from past shows too—about labels, sports, entertainment, fashion, food, hair, music—just tons of stuff that kids should know.

http://www.screen.com/streetcents.html

Andrea Bonilla, 13

Find Out How!

Effect: A dime is borrowed from a spectator and its date is noted. The dime joins a quarter in the magician's hand. The magician then places the dime into his pocket and as if by magic the same dime reappears in his hand with the quarter. The dime is returned and the date is noted to be the correct one.

FIZBin's Young Magician's Magazine
http://www.tiac.net/users /rjf/fizbin.html

Oksana Talks!

Q: How does it feel to be a gold medalist and beat Nancy Kerrigan?

A: You know, I'm not really the kind of person who likes to compete. Of course, I like to compete, but you know, it's life. She skated very well. I saw her performance on videotape. It wasn't my choice. I didn't choose to win. The judges made the decision. And having a gold medal, it's unbelievable. I worked for that my whole life. And I have that surprise. I have that medal.

Interview with Oksana Baiul
Sports Illustrated for Kids
http://pathfinder.com/SIFK

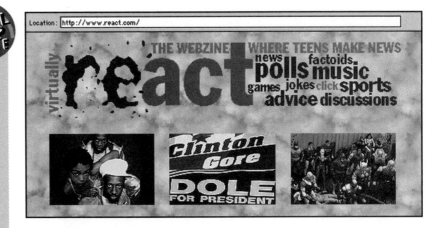

Location: http://www.react.com/

Surf Virtually React

Surf Virtually React is where teens make news. It is a colorful and fun site that is well worth a look. It includes everything from games, to play on long road trips, to the sports page. One of its features is Field and Screen, a section that has film reviews, videos, music, TV, and sports. Another is Everyday Heroes, which focuses on the achievements of everyday teens.
http://www.react.com
Philip Reilly, 12

TIME for Kids

This page was very educational and boring. If you are a kid and care about what's happening in the world, this is a neat page. But most kids don't really care, so this page is kind of lame. It has news and a cartoon, but the cartoon was not funny. So, if you like news, it's good; if you don't, stay away.
http://pathfinder.com/TFK/index.html
Emily Malloch, 11

YES Mag for Kids

This page was fun and educational. It had a quiz of things that we never really think about. It has some cool projects that you can do right at home. It also has some news, but not so much that you could fall asleep. This is a great page to learn and have fun at.

http://www.islandnet.com/~yesmag

Emily Malloch, 11

Location: http://www.islandnet.com/~yesmag/

YES MAG
canada's Science Magazine for Kids

Sci & Tech News

Hands-on Projects

Brain Bumpers

Feature Stories

How Does That World

Reviews By Kids

YES Mag -- On Paper

YES Camps of Canada

What Did You Think?

Celebrate National S&T Week – Win Prizes

On your way out? Try our links

Hanging with Spiderman

COOL KID SITE

"Spiderman is my hero. We would swing on a web. After that we would stop the bad guys. We would stop Venom. Then we would catch Carnedge. After that we would swing around. Spiderman is my favorite. Then the day would be over."

Caden, 2nd grade, Dover, Oklahoma from *The Looking Glass Gazette*

http://www.cowboy.net /~mharper/LGG/V5N4 /CCade.html

Build Your Own Web Site

With so many kids out there making up their own home pages you must be thinking—well, how hard can it be? Here are some places to go for help

Web Cheats!

"There are several 'tricky' things you can do to try to get your URL listed higher or more times on a search engine results page. We are listing these alternatives, but are in no way recommending them as these Web site promotion methods may be viewed as 'cheating' by some members of the Internet community. In fact, some of the search engines are starting to penalize people that use these tricks."

Submit It
http://submit-it.permalink
.com/submit-it

The Epicenter

I wish I'd known about this site sooner. You will have an easy time making a home page if you go here to get help. It is a site about disaster warnings and weather but also has good Web stuff. Be sure you go to the Maze from the Fun and Games icon. It is a cool adventure through rooms where you can go different ways to try to get through. Don't be afraid to go to some of the Web help sites. You can download good stuff from them.

http://theepicenter.com/webdev.html

Amy Schroeder, 10

Randy's Icon and Image Bazaar

Do you have a home page on the Internet, or have you considered making one? If so, you should definitely visit Randy's Icon and Image Bazaar. Here, you'll find an endless list of icons, backgrounds, images, and more to use for free to brighten up your Internet creation.

http://www.infi.net/~rdralph/icons

Melissa Edwards, 14

The Hot Dog Web Editor

The Best. Get help here! I do. I downloaded some nice backgrounds from a link on this page. There are lots of links here, so try them and you will get the stuff you need. My dad uses this software and it helps us design pages fast. You will make this a top bookmark, and wear it out. Backgrounds, icons, page dividers, tips, tools—it's all available here. Can you tell I like it? Expect to spend a half hour or more here, it will seem like a minute.

http://wco.com/~linnins/tpresop.htm

Amy Schroeder, 10

WWW Viewer Test Page

This page is one of the most useful on the WWW. It gives you a chance to test your viewers in categories such as video, audio, html, vrml, and images. No graphics on this site, but it does offer in-depth explanations. An essential site to see when wandering the Web.

http://www/WWWtest.html

Jeff Little, 13

It All Adds Up!

Nice page. It is very simple. It has everything you need to know about making a Web page counter. It has a creation page, a trouble-shooting page, thumbnails you can put on your page of the Web counter pages logo to acknowledge them, and an **FAQ** for all of your Web counter questions. It also has a feedback page for your questions and comments.

Creating a Web-Counter
http://www.digits.com
/create.html

- WEB c⊙u∩ʈe⌐™ Interlaced GIF. Width 216. Height 23. Solid background.
- WEB c⊙u∩ʈe⌐™ Interlaced GIF. Width 267. Height 28. Transparent background.
- WEB c⊙u∩ʈe⌐™ Interlaced GIF. Width 267. Height 28. Solid background.
- WEB c⊙u∩ʈe⌐™ Interlaced GIF. Width 330. Height 36. Transparent background.
- WEB c⊙u∩ʈe⌐™ Interlaced GIF. Width 330. Height 36. Solid background.
- WEB c⊙u∩ʈe⌐™ Interlaced GIF. Width 408. Height 45. Transparent background.
- WEB c⊙u∩ʈe⌐™ Interlaced GIF. Width 408. Height 45. Solid background.

Adult FAQ

1. Why should I put my child online?

Recent studies show that people who spend more time online watch less TV. That's good news for kids, because this new medium is extremely educational. In the course of researching this book, we discovered that kids online spend a lot of time writing each other email, programming their own home pages, and finding information about anything in the world that interests them. Long after school's out, they're still busy reading, writing, and searching for information. That can't hurt them. It also can't hurt them to be familiar with the medium that promises to be the library, marketplace, and meeting place of the twenty-first century.

2. They have a library at school, isn't that enough?

School libraries face shrinking budgets. Town and city libraries face similar difficulties. Going online yourself ensures that your child need never be limited by teachers with no time to answer a question or by a library with out-of-date books. As 13-year-old Kellie Vaughn of Huntsville, Ala. says, "It's like a huge encyclopedia with pictures that talk, sing, and do most anything. If you have a question on anything, and I do mean anything, the Internet has the answer."

3. But I have a girl. Isn't the Internet mostly a boy thing?

Girls love the Internet. With the advent of the Internet, the computer is no longer just a toy for nerdy boys: it's an easel, it's a library, and it's a phone. As we discovered while researching this book, girls are spending a lot of time online chatting with each other, reading each other's stories, and sending each other email. They're making friends, too. For example, a NetKid in Florida told a friend in the Philippines to write to us to ask to become a reviewer, and one of our NetKids in England recommended a girl in California she thought would be good. That Californian, 13-year-old Carol Scott, says, "The Internet is GREAT for girls especially! Who says computers are just for guys? Girls are on the Internet, too! There are TONS of online girls' sites, and tons of girls' clubs, too! And this may be strange coming from guy-centered technology, but there are a LOT more Web sites for girls 6–18 than for boys 6–8! That's cool!"

4. Should I sign up for a direct connection or an online service?

It used to be that online services were a much easier way to start on the Internet than dial-up direct access. This is no longer true. The main reason to sign on with an online service now is if you think the services they offer are worth the premium you'll pay. There are great things on the online services for kids, but there are also many great things for kids on the Web. Access to the Internet now hovers at around $20 per month for unlimited use, which can work out to be a much cheaper alternative than the per-hour services.

5. What kind of computer works best?

We recommend a 486 class PC or better, or a fairly new Macintosh. In any case, try to get something that's equipped for multimedia. The Web is being filled with color and sound, and you and your child will enjoy surfing much more if you can take advantage of all those capabilities. You should also get a 28.8Kbps modem. They're a bit more expensive than 14.4Kbps, but twice as fast.

6. How can I protect my child on the Internet?

Several screening programs are available that work something like the V chip, but the risk you run in installing one of them is that in trying to protect your child you may awaken the hacker within. There is nothing like a locked door to encourage curiosity. A less high-tech but ultimately more reliable approach may be to look over your kid's shoulder once in a while and to talk about what he or she's been up to online.

Net Nanny
http://www.netnanny.com

- Total parental control. This software lets you monitor the kids' computer use and define what you want them to be able to access. Violations trigger a shutdown of either the application or the computer.

- Monitors all Internet and PC activity online or off, including TCP/IP streams, Web browsers, newsgroups, FTPs, IRC, email, and BBSs, as well as all offline Windows or DOS applications.

- Features full Internet filtering capability and controlled access to local PC files, drives, loading of unauthorized diskettes and CD-ROMS, and menu commands.

- Works with PC running MS-DOS v3.3, Windows v3.1, or Windows 95.

- Costs 39^{95.}$

- Free evaluation copy available at this site.

Cyber Patrol
http://www.cyberpatrol.com

- Monitors, filters, and blocks all Internet access.
- CyberNOT Block List (subsequent subscriptions cost 29^{95} a year).
- Requires the CyberNOT Block List of access-denied URLs, which is updated regularly; ChatGuard feature controls chatroom access.
- Works with Macintosh or Windows.
- Costs 29^{95} for registered software plus a three-month subscription to the CyberNOT list.
- Free demos of Cyber Patrol 3.0 and 2.11 are downloadable at this site.

CYBERsitter
http://www.solidoak.com/cybersit.htm

- Monitors all Internet activity, including attempts to access blocked material.
- Filters "bad sites" and phrases.
- Works with Windows 95 or Windows 3.1x.
- Costs 39^{95}.
- Free trial version downloadable from this site.

Tattle-Tale
http://www.pond.com/~pearlsft

Keep track of the kids' Internet use or restrict access at a level you control.

- Monitors all Internet activity including sites visited and information exchanged.

- Reports include quick links to the sites visited so parents can verify their content.
- Works with Windows 3.1 or later, Windows 95, or Windows NT.
- Costs 29^{95}.

7. My kid loves to chat, but I'm worried about her chatting away with all these strangers. What's the best way to handle that?

Many kids like to chat online, both with each other and with grownups. Chat rooms can be a great part of being on the Internet, but try to give your youngster some guidelines about what's OK to talk about and what's not OK. You may also want to look over shoulders occasionally to make sure everything is all right. If you do the navigating in your house, look for rooms where discussion is moderated, especially if you have little surfers who can't fend for themselves yet. Some chat channels, such as The Palace, have virtual bouncers to make sure things don't get out of hand. There are kid-only and kid-safe chat rooms around, and we've included some of those in this book, but a chat room is by its nature more unstable than a Web site, and no reviewer in the world can guarantee who is going to be where at a given time. Be a little cautious.

Index

Index

Index

Index

Kids' Credits

We would like to express a huge **THANK-YOU** to all the kids from all over the world who participated in *NetKids*. For those of you whose work didn't appear in this book, keep your browsers pointed at www.ypn.com, because we plan to use all your reviews!

Sarah Alderdice, 10
Cranfor, New Jersey, USA

Morgan Balavage, 12
Redding, California, USA

Alexandra Barsk, 12
New York, New York, USA

Andrea Bonilla, 13
Stony Creek, Ontario, Canada

Stephanie Co, 10
Manila, Philippines

Nicholas Cofranesco, 14
Springfield, Vermont, USA

Joe Conrad, 13
Owosso, Michigan, USA

Derya Davenport, 11
Ankara, Turkey

Melissa Edwards, 14
Memphis, Tennesee, USA

Erin Fleege, 13
Hartford, Wisconsin, USA

Ian Grant, 14
South Dartmouth,
Massachusetts, USA

Danielle Jacovelli, 11
Wagga Wagga, New South
Wales, Australia

Alex Landback, 10
Tampa, Florida, USA

Bronwyn Lee, 12
Sydney, New South Wales,
Australia

Nigel Lee, 13
Wanchai, Hong Kong

David Lindsay, 11
Calgary, Alberta, Canada

Samantha Lipton, 12
New York, New York, USA

Jeff Little, 13
Sault Sainte Marie, Ontario,
Canada

Ai Kurobi, 12
Tokyo, Japan

Emily Malloch, 11
New Berlin, New York, USA

Kelsey Mays, 11
Refugio, Texas, USA

Adam Michaels, 13
Lincoln Beach, Ontario,
Canada

Keith Miller, 8
Reston, Virginia, USA

Hayley Morgan, 12
Birmingham, England

Maryangela Moutoussis, 12
New York, New York, USA

Rachel Prior, 11
Alice Springs, Northern
Territory, Australia

David Reilly, 10
Wolverton, Milton Keynes,
England

Philip Reilly, 12
Wolverton, Milton Keynes,
England

Alexis Riordan, 12
New York, New York, USA

Kelly Roman, 11
Princetown, New Jersey, USA

Leslie Safier, 12
Youngstown, Ohio, USA

Tweba Sargeant, 12
New York, New York, USA

David Sawchak, 7
Charleston, South Carolina,
USA

Amy Schroeder, 10
Lompoc, California, USA

Carol Scott, 13
Hawthorne, California, USA

Nicole Sleeth, 10
Ottawa, Ontario, Canada

Nykki-Lynn Smelser, 10
London, Ontario, Canada

Katie Tandler, 13
Midlothian, Virginia, USA

Jillian Tellez, 9
Winter Spring, Florida, USA

Katie Van Winkle, 11
Austin, Texas, USA

Kellie Vaughn, 13
Huntsville, Alabama, USA

Andrew Vega, 7
Long Island, New York , USA

Elizabeth Wolff, 12
New York, New York, USA

Susanna Wolff, 8
New York, New York, USA

Beth Yankee, 11
Tallahassee, Florida, USA

WOLFF NEW MEDIA

Vice President, Associate Publisher: Carol Lappin
Vice President, Marketing: Jay Sears
Advertising Director: Michael Domican
Advertising Sales: Eric Oldfield, Bob Treuber
Marketing Coordinator: Amy Winger
Marketing Assistant: Joanna Harper

YPN Development Producer: Jonathan Bellack
Associate Directory Editor: Richard Egan
YPN Managing Editor: Mila Shulkleper
YPN Producers: Molly Confer, Rachel Greene,
Alison Grippo, Jonathan Spooner

Systems Administrator: Jonathan Chapman
Database Administrator: Graham Young
Database Technician: Toby Spinks

Administrative Assistant: Ann Peters

WOLFF NEW MEDIA LLC

Michael Wolff
President

James M. Morouse
Executive Vice President

Alison Anthoine
Vice President

Joseph Cohen
Chief Financial Officer

Image Credits

Dennis Rodman, p. 96, http://www.texas.net/users/pmagal/; Steve Young, p. 100, http://www.ece.orst.edu/~bevans/sy.html; Saddled horse jumping, p. 102, http://www.umd.umich.edu/~reasons/rodeo/; Tiny horses, p. 103, http://www-cgi.cnn.com/WORLD/9511/tibet _pony; Multiple wrestlers, p. 105, http://www.ai2a.net/~sloride/; Villa Soccer Club, p. 108, http://www.cybergoal.com/soccer/team.html; Quattro soccer ball, p. 109, http://www.inferdata.com/quattro-soccer-balls/std/index.html; Swim meet, p. 110, http://www.oxy.edu/departments/athletics/swimming/pictures.htm; Cliff diving, p. 111, http://www.ith.ca/desk/station/acapulco.html; Inline skater, p. 112, http://www.skatecity.com/C+W/; Inline skater #151, http://www.seas.smu.edu/~justin/inline.html; Inline skater on a a hand rail, p. 114, http://www.seas.smu.edu/~justin/inline.html; Helmet-less inline skater, p. 115, http://www.seas.smu.edu/~justin/inline.html; 1939 Nash auto, p. 119, http://www.auschron.com/issues/vol15/issue23/cols.smartypamts.html; Lamborghini, p. 119, http://www.lamborghini.com; Charles Lindbergh, p. 120, http://zeta.broonale.co.uk/austria/lindbergh.html; Amelia Earhart map, p. 121, Amelia Earhart in suit, p. 121, http://www.ionet.net/~jellenc/ae_celb.html; The Titanic, p. 122, http://www.lib.virginia.edu/cataloging/vnp/titanic/giant.gif; Maritime flags, p. 123, http://www.nav.com/ports/game.htm; Charging train, p. 124, http://www.tcd.net/~mevans19/images/siltrain.jpg; Coleman train, p. 125, http://www.infinet.com/~colemanc/Bin/who_aug.gif; New York City subway map, p. 125, http://subway.k2nesoft.com/routemap/manhattan.gif; The Eiffel Tower, p. 126, http://sinsite.unc.edu/louvre; Cleveland's Rock and Roll Hall of Fame, p. 127, http://www.rockhall.com; World Sufari, p. 128, http://supersurf.com/fun.htm; Building with steps, p. 129, http://www.coolsite.com/arworld.html; Branching river, p. 129, http://www.nationalgeographic.com/ngs/mags/ng_online/photography/ph_sep96/0179.html; Virtual Monopoly, p. 132, http://www.monopoly.com/Images/; Chess piece, http://www.sojourn.com/~sean/web/cheshist.html; Mortal Kombat screenshot, p. 134, http://www.directnet.com; Barbie pics, p. 136, http://darwin.clas.virginia.edu/~tsawyer/barbie/barb.html; Annette dolls, p. 137, http://dspace.dial.pipex.com/town/square/fj09/dolls.html; Slide puzzle, p. 138, http://www.bu.edu/games/puzzle; Lego homes and forts, p. 141, http://www.lego.com; Alice in Wonderland illustrations, p. 142, http://www.cstone.net/library/alice/carroll.html; Scary monster, p. 145, http://www.scholastic.com/public/Goosebumps; Winnie the Pooh, p. 146, http://worldaccess.com/pooh/welcome.html; Flying saucer, p. 150, http://www.io.org/~dnewton/ufo.html; Independence Day, p. 150, http://www.id4.com; Computerized alien head, p. 151, http://www.iufo.org; Map of the Bermuda Triangle, p. 154, http://tigger.cc.iuc.edu/~toby-g/tri.html; Bigfoot, p. 155, http://www.teleport.com/~tbrp; Jessica Dubroff, p. 161, http://www.azc.com/client/enn2/kidsnews.htm; Girls Only sign, p. 162, http://www.davelash.com/amber/girlpage.html; Multiple electronic postcards, p. 163, http://postcards.www.media.mit.edu/Postcards; Palace screenshots, p. 165, http://www.thepalace.com; Magician and coins, p. 167, http://www.magical.com/secrets/; Spiderman illustration, p. 169, http://www.cowboy.net/~mharper/LGG/V5N4/CCade.html

Cover Image Credits